D0172300

PENGUIN

ARKANA

ARKANA
ZEN SOUP

Laurence G. Boldt is a writer and career consultant based in the San Francisco Bay area. He is the author of *Zen and the Art of Making a Living* (Arkana, 1993) and *How to Find the Work You Love* (Arkana, 1996).

LAURENCE G. BOLDT ✍

ZEN SOUP

Tasty Morsels of Wisdom from Great Minds
East & West

PENGUIN · ARKANA

ARKANA
Published by the Penguin Group
Penguin Putnam Inc., 375 Hudson Street,
New York, New York 10014, U.S.A.
Penguin Books Ltd, 27 Wrights Lane, London W8 5TZ, England
Penguin Books Australia Ltd, Ringwood, Victoria, Australia
Penguin Books Canada Ltd, 10 Alcorn Avenue,
Toronto, Ontario, Canada M4V 3B2
Penguin Books (N.Z.) Ltd, 182–190 Wairau Road,
Auckland 10, New Zealand

Penguin Books Ltd, Registered Offices:
Harmondsworth, Middlesex, England

First published in Arkana 1997

3 5 7 9 10 8 6 4

LIBRARY OF CONGRESS CATALOGING
IN PUBLICATION DATA
Boldt, Laurence G.
Zen soup : tasty morsels of wisdom from great minds East & West /
Laurence G. Boldt.
p. cm.
Includes index.
ISBN 0 14 019560 2 (pbk.)
1. Zen Buddhism—Quotations, maxims, etc. I. Title.
BQ9267.B65   1997
294.3'927—dc21   97–5190

Printed in the United States of America
Set in Fournier
Designed by Fritz Metsch

To Kim and Susan

A book of quotes such as this is a collection of highly distilled thoughts. According to the *I Ching*, that most profound classic of Chinese literature, thoughts are spirits. I am confident that reading these quotes will put you in the company of good spirits. For me, many have become old and trusted friends. At various points in my life, they have helped me to arouse courage, confirm direction, persist in effort, let go of attachment, and have a good laugh at myself. I am happy to be able to share them with you and hope that you will be blessed by them, as I have been.

This book is organized around twenty-five aspects, or qualities, associated with the Zen tradition. After a brief introductory essay comes a collection of quotes that illuminate each quality. While many come out of the Zen literature or other Eastern sources, most are from our own Western tradition. The diversity of sources highlights the timeless and universal nature of these principles.

Of course, to speak of Zen in terms of thoughts or qualities is to miss it altogether. Yet what we think *does* make a difference. Thoughts can point us in the right direction or just as easily lead us astray. In the words of a familiar Zen saying: "In a thought of Buddha, I embrace Nirvana; in a thought of evil, I open the Gates of Hell." It is my sincere hope that these thoughts may serve to remind you of your own Buddha nature.

CONTENTS

Preface vii

BE HERE NOW I

BEGINNER'S MIND 6

COURAGE 17

RIGHT THINKING 28

REALITY 36

RESPONSIBILITY 44

BE YOURSELF 54

WORK 64

CREATIVITY 72

CONTENTS

HUMOR 79

SELF-CONFIDENCE 86

COMPASSION 93

JOY 102

DISCIPLINE 110

WONDER 118

THE GAME OF LIFE 123

INTEGRITY 129

SELFLESS SERVICE 137

THE ART OF ZEN 146

PERSEVERANCE 152

LETTING GO 159

MEDITATION 164

MINDFULNESS 171

ENLIGHTENMENT 176

EVERYDAY ZEN 183

Index 191

ZEN SOUP

BE

HERE

NOW

If Zen is telling us anything, it is to be here now, to live in this moment. Simple enough. So what stops us? To live in the moment, we must go out of our minds. The mind, with its guilt and resentment about the past and its fears and hopes for the future, the mind that confuses thoughts about people, things, and events with the people, things, and events themselves—must be transcended. Out of the mind and into direct, immediate experience—this is the message of Zen.

Zen masters have often used dramatic techniques, including verbal insults, physical violence, and absurd theatrics, to jolt students out of mental preoccupation and thrust them back into the moment. Zen is forever shouting: Wake up! Wake up! Wake Up! Stop the mind already! Be here! It helps to sit still and meditate. Yet Zen is even more concerned with being "here now" in the midst of activity. Again and again, Zen teachers exhort the principle of *mo chich ch'u,* or "going ahead without hesitation." Just do what you are doing without thinking about it. Just be where you are without holding on or running away. Give up judging and spectating and dive into this moment. If you can't find it here, where will you go to find it? And when?

❧

This time, like all times, is a very good one, if we but know what to do with it.

—RALPH WALDO EMERSON

❧

Paradise is where I am.   —VOLTAIRE

❧

In walking, just walk. In sitting, just sit. Above all, don't wobble.   —YUN-MEN

❧

If you want to be happy, be.

—HENRY DAVID THOREAU

❧

The only way to make sense out of change is to plunge into it, move with it, and join the dance.

—ALAN WATTS

❧

I think that what we're seeking is an experience of being alive, so that our life experiences on the purely physical plane will have resonances within our own innermost being and reality, so that we actually feel the rapture of being alive.

—JOSEPH CAMPBELL

❧

The Tao is near and people seek it far away.

—MENCIUS

❧

Real generosity toward the future consists in giving all to what is present.   —ALBERT CAMUS

❧

May you live all the days of your life.

—JONATHAN SWIFT

❧

I exist as I am, that is enough.

—WALT WHITMAN

❧

The present is great with the future.

—GOTTFRIED LEIBNITZ

❧

When one is engaged in a favorite pursuit or a subject absorbingly interesting, the normal conception of labor or time and artificial social distinctions disappear from the mind.　　　—G. KOIZUMI

❧

Is not life a thousand times too short for us to bore ourselves?　　　—FRIEDRICH NIETZSCHE

❧

What you see is what you get.　　　—FLIP WILSON

❧

We look backward too much and we look forward too much; thus we miss the only eternity of which we can be absolutely sure—the eternal present, for it is always now.   —WILLIAM PHELPS

❧

To be where we are, and to become what we are capable of becoming, is the only end in life.

—ROBERT LOUIS STEVENSON

BEGINNER'S

MIND

The ultimate beginner's mind is that of the child. Children learn so rapidly because they are neither afraid of not knowing nor convinced that they already know what they don't. The rest of us could take a lesson. After a certain age, many of us no longer seek out new knowledge or experience. On the contrary, we take pains to avoid the exposure of ignorance and the ridicule we fear will accompany it. In our defensiveness, we act as though we know, even when we know we don't. When we love and accept ourselves as we are, we engage in the vulnerable act of learning without the fear of looking foolish. We can profit from the knowledge and experience of others because we love ourselves enough to put our desire to grow ahead of defending our ignorance.

The beginner's mind applies not only to learning new skills, activities, or information but to all we think we know about life. Many of us walk around with deeply ingrained beliefs that limit our experience. For example, we think: "If things get too good, something bad will happen," or "You can't really trust people," or "You can't really do or have what you want in life." Of course, we can insist on these kinds of beliefs, select out supportive incidents from the past, and build cases for why they are so; but this only shuts the door on new experience. As only an empty cup can be filled, so only a heart emptied of the pride of what it thinks it knows can be open to new experience and receive the gifts of wisdom. When we embrace the humility to meet life head-on, without the baggage of what we think we know, we make room for ourselves to grow.

❧

To know that you do not know is the best. To
pretend to know when you do not know is a
disease. —LAO-TZU

❧

It's what you learn after you know it all that
counts. —JOHN WOODEN

❧

The trouble with most of us is that we know too
much that ain't so. —MARK TWAIN

❧

The chief object of education is not to learn things
but to unlearn things. —G. K. CHESTERTON

❧

Who has no faults? To err and yet be able to
correct it is best of all. —YÜAN-WU

❧

Real learning comes about when the competitive
spirit has ceased . . . This is true not only of competition with others, but competition with yourself.
—J. KRISHNAMURTI

❧

The world is our school for spiritual discovery.

—PAUL BRUNTON

❧

He who Knows what he is Told, must know a Lot
of Things that Are Not So.

—ARTHUR GUITERMAN

❧

He who can copy can do.

—LEONARDO DA VINCI

❧

The great end of education is to discipline rather
than to furnish the mind; to train it to the use of its
own powers, rather than fill it with the accumula-
tion of others.　　　　　—TYRON EDWARDS

❧

Education is not filling a bucket but lighting a fire.

—WILLIAM BUTLER YEATS

❧

Everyone is ignorant, only in different subjects.

—WILL ROGERS

❦

The more I learn, the more I realize I don't know.

—ALBERT EINSTEIN

❦

Man's capacities have never been measured, nor are we to judge of what he can do by any precedent, so little has been tried. —HENRY DAVID THOREAU

❦

Learning is the very essence of humility. . . .

—J. KRISHNAMURTI

❦

Is not indeed every man a student, and do not all things exist for the student's behoof?

—RALPH WALDO EMERSON

❦

The only person who is educated is the one who has learned how to learn . . . and change.

—CARL ROGERS

❦

In antiquity men studied for their own sake; nowadays men study for the sake of impressing others.

—CONFUCIUS

❦

A little learning is a dangerous thing; drink deep or taste not the Pierian spring.   —ALEXANDER POPE

❦

Experience is the best of school masters, only the school fees are heavy.   —THOMAS CARLYLE

❦

Tell me, I'll forget. Show me, I may remember. But involve me and I'll understand.

—CHINESE PROVERB

❦

Anyone who stops learning is old, whether twenty or eighty. Anyone who keeps learning today is young. The greatest thing in life is to keep your mind young.   —HENRY FORD

❧

What is now proved was once only imagin'd.
——WILLIAM BLAKE

❧

Growth is the only evidence of life.
——CARDINAL NEWMAN

❧

When we see men of worth, we should think of equaling them; when we see men of contrary character, we should turn inwards and examine ourselves.
——CONFUCIUS

❧

Is there anyone so wise as to learn by the experience of others?
——VOLTAIRE

❧

The great man is he who does not lose his child's heart.
——MENCIUS

❧

A man only learns in two ways, one by reading, and the other by association with smarter people.

—WILL ROGERS

❧

Experience keeps a dear school, but fools will learn in no other.   —BENJAMIN FRANKLIN

❧

A man should never be ashamed to own he has been wrong, which is but saying, in other words, that he is wiser today than he was yesterday.

—ALEXANDER POPE

❧

Example is the school of mankind, and they will learn at no other.   —EDMUND BURKE

❧

Much learning does not teach a man to have intelligence.   —HERACLITUS

❧

We can be knowledgeable with another man's knowledge, but we cannot be wise with another man's wisdom. —MICHEL DE MONTAIGNE

✿

A person's errors are his portals of discovery.

—JAMES JOYCE

✿

A man must have a certain amount of intelligent ignorance to get anywhere.

—CHARLES KETTERING

✿

It's better to know nothing than to know what ain't so. —JOSH BILLINGS

✿

Men stumble over the truth from time to time, but most pick themselves up and hurry off as if nothing happened. —WINSTON CHURCHILL

✿

Youth is a quality, and if you have it, you never
lose it. ——FRANK L. WRIGHT

✿

Genius is nothing more or less than childhood re-
covered by will, a childhood now equipped for self-
expression with an adult's capacities.

——CHARLES BAUDELAIRE

✿

Men are wise in proportion not to their experience,
but in their capacity for experience.

——GEORGE BERNARD SHAW

✿

I am not ashamed to confess that I am ignorant of
what I do not know. ——CICERO

✿

I am defeated and know it if I meet any human
being from which I find myself unable to learn anything. ——GEORGE HERBERT PALMER

✿

Personally I am always ready to learn, although I do not always like being taught.

—WINSTON CHURCHILL

❦

Everybody wants to be somebody; nobody wants to grow.　　　　　—JOHANN GOETHE

❦

In the beginner's mind there are many possibilities, but in the expert's there are few.

—SHUNRYU SUZUKI

COURAGE

We have no greater enemy than fear. It hems us in, sucks the joy out of life, and leaves us with disgust for ourselves. Nothing of importance can be undertaken or achieved without facing, challenging, and finally mastering fear. If it takes great courage to attempt and accomplish things of real merit, it takes even more to be what we truly are.

Friedrich Nietzsche described a threefold process in the maturation of consciousness. He said that in the first stage, we are like a *camel* bending down to have hoisted upon us the load of social conditioning, habit, and convention. In the second stage, we are like a *lion* roaring against the "thou shalts" of society. Only after we have completed the work of the lion do we become the *child*, which is to say, a fully human being, capable of spontaneously, intuitively, and competently responding to the world. The courage of the lion is the courage to find your own path in life. It requires that you examine the conventions, ideals, and programs of society, as well as the habits and routines you have unconsciously accumulated, and determine for yourself what to accept and what to reject.

The measure of our courage is reflected in the vision of life we choose and in how much it takes for us to become discouraged. Too often we think of ourselves as weak candles that can be blown out by the slightest wind of frustration or disappointment. How much better to say: "I will become a bonfire and dare the world to put me out."

ॐ

What a new face courage puts on everything.

—RALPH WALDO EMERSON

ॐ

Courage is the price that life exacts for granting peace.

—AMELIA EARHART

❦

Be not afraid of life. Believe that life is worth
living, and your belief will help create the fact.
— WILLIAM JAMES

❦

To see what is right and not do it is want of
courage.   — CONFUCIUS

❦

Courage is grace under pressure.
— ERNEST HEMINGWAY

❦

Every society honors its live conformists and its
dead troublemakers.   — MIGNON MCLAUGHLIN

❦

I believe that anyone can conquer fear by doing the
things he fears to do . . .
— ELEANOR ROOSEVELT

❧

A man with outward courage dares to die
A man with inward courage dares to live.

—LAO-TZU

❧

There is nothing with which every man is so afraid
as getting to know how enormously much he is
capable of doing and becoming.

—SÖREN KIERKEGAARD

❧

Nothing is terrible except fear itself.

—FRANCIS BACON

❧

Alas! the fearful Unbelief is unbelief in yourself.

—THOMAS CARLYLE

❧

There are costs and risks to a program of action,
but they are far less than the long range risks and
costs of comfortable inaction.

—JOHN F. KENNEDY

❧

Fortune favors the audacious. —ERASMUS

❧

No one knows what he can do until he tries.

—SYRUS

❧

There are three essentials to leadership: humility, clarity, and courage. —FUSHAN YUAN

❧

Let me not pray to be sheltered from dangers but to be fearless in facing them. Let me not beg for the stilling of my pain but for the heart to conquer it. —TAGORE

❧

There's nothing in the world so admired as a man who knows how to bear unhappiness with courage.

—SENECA

❧

Bravery never goes out of style.

—WILLIAM THACKERAY

❧

Our demons are our own limitations, which shut us off from the realization of the ubiquity of the spirit . . . each of these demons is conquered in a vision quest. —JOSEPH CAMPBELL

❧

Life shrinks or expands in proportion to one's courage. —ANAÏS NIN

❧

He that hath nothing is frightened of nothing.

—ENGLISH PROVERB

❧

A warrior must only take care that his spirit is never broken. —SHISSAI

❧

Fortune and love befriend the bold. —OVID

❧

Only those who will risk going too far can possibly find out how far one can go.

——T. S. ELIOT

❧

We must dare, and dare again, and go on daring.

——GEORGES DANTON

❧

The greatest obstacle to being heroic is the doubt whether one may not be going to prove one's self a fool; the truest heroism is, to resist the doubt; and the profoundest wisdom, to know when it ought to be resisted, and when to be obeyed.

——NATHANIEL HAWTHORNE

❧

It is difficulties that show what men are.

——EPICTETUS

❧

Our doubts are traitors and make us lose the good
we oft might win by fearing to attempt.

—SHAKESPEARE

❧

Fear always springs from ignorance.

—RALPH WALDO EMERSON

❧

It is only by risking our persons from one hour to
another that we live at all. And often enough our
faith beforehand in an uncertified result is the only
thing that makes the result come true.

—WILLIAM JAMES

❧

Has fear ever held a man back from anything he
really wanted, or a woman either?

—GEORGE BERNARD SHAW

❧

It is necessary to any originality to have the
courage to be an amateur.

—WALLACE STEVENS

❧

Change and growth take place when a person has risked himself and dares to become involved with experimenting with his own life.

——HERBERT OTTO

❧

No work of love will flourish out of guilt, fear, or hollowness of heart, just as no valid plans for the future can be made by those who have no capacity for living now. ——ALAN WATTS

❧

The worst fear is the fear of living.

——THEODORE ROOSEVELT

❧

Courage is not the absence of fear, but rather the judgment that something else is more important than fear. ——AMBROSE REDMOON

❧

Only the brave know how to forgive . . . A
coward never forgave; it is not in his nature.

—LAURENCE STERNE

❧

Life is either a daring adventure, or nothing.

—HELEN KELLER

❧

Discontent is want of self-reliance; it is infirmity of
will.　　　　　—RALPH WALDO EMERSON

❧

A man of courage is also full of faith.　　—CICERO

❧

Whatever you do or dream you can do—begin it.
Boldness has genius and power and magic in it.

—JOHANN GOETHE

❧

The principal act of courage is to endure and with-
stand dangers doggedly rather than to attack them.

—THOMAS AQUINAS

❦

Courage is the first of human qualities because it is
a quality which guarantees the others.

—WINSTON CHURCHILL

RIGHT

THINKING

Right thinking is a critical element of the Buddhist way of enlightenment known as "The Noble Eightfold Path." "Thoughts," as Emerson put it, "rule the world" for the simple reason that thoughts determine feelings and actions. We can think ourselves into happiness or a deep depression. We can think ourselves into health or illness. We can think ourselves into peace of mind or a raging fury. We can think ourselves into a narrow, limited world characterized by procrastination and paralysis, or we can think ourselves into a noble, creative life and the actions that give it shape and substance. If we only take care of our thoughts, our feelings and actions will take care of themselves.

For better or worse, we give to others the fruits of our own thinking. By the same token, we are influenced by the thinking of those with whom we associate. It certainly helps to make friends with people who have made friends with their own minds. Observe people who are chronically bored or depressed, and you will invariably find that they dwell on negative thoughts. Observe people who are consistently happy, creative, and productive, and you will find remarkable similarities in the quality of their thinking.

By our thinking, we create our individual and collective experience of reality. Changing our thinking for the better improves the quality of our own lives, and in so doing, uplifts all around us.

❧

Not he is great who can alter matter, but he who can alter my state of mind.

—RALPH WALDO EMERSON

❧

For one who has conquered the mind, the mind is the best of friends. But for one who has failed to do so, his very mind will be his greatest enemy.

—BHAGAVAD-GITA

❧

One comes to be of just such stuff as that on which
the mind is set.   ——UPANISHADS

❧

The universe is change; our life is what our
thoughts make it.   ——MARCUS AURELIUS

❧

As the physically weak man can make himself
strong by careful and patient training, so the man
of weak thoughts can make them strong by exercis-
ing himself in right thinking.   ——JAMES ALLEN

❧

Bless relaxes, damn braces.   ——WILLIAM BLAKE

❧

The idea that is not dangerous is unworthy of
being called an idea at all.   ——ELBERT HUBBARD

❧

We are what we think. All that we are arises with our thoughts. With our thoughts we make the world. —BUDDHA

❧

Human beings can alter their lives by altering their attitudes of mind. —WILLIAM JAMES

❧

If you refuse to accept anything but the best out of life, you very often get it. —SOMERSET MAUGHAM

❧

The mind is the great leveler of all things; human thought is the process by which human ends are ultimately answered. —DANIEL WEBSTER

❧

As he thinketh in his heart, so is he. —PROVERBS 23:7

❧

It is a very great thing to be able to think as you like; but after all, an important question remains: what you think. —MATTHEW ARNOLD

❧

Nurture your minds with great thoughts. To believe in the heroic makes heroes.

—BENJAMIN DISRAELI

❧

All that a man achieves and all that he fails to achieve is the direct result of his own thoughts.

—JAMES ALLEN

❧

All wrong-doing arises because of mind. If mind is transformed can wrong-doing remain? —BUDDHA

❧

The ills from which we are suffering have had their seat in the very foundation of human thought.

—TEILHARD DE CHARDIN

❧

It is the mind that maketh good or ill, that maketh wretch or happy, rich or poor.

—EDMUND SPENSER

❧

Your own mind is a sacred enclosure into which nothing harmful can enter except by your permission. —ARNOLD BENNETT

❧

A man is about as happy as he makes up his mind to be. —ABRAHAM LINCOLN

❧

Since wars begin in the minds of men, it is in the minds of men that we have to erect the ramparts of peace. —UNESCO CHARTER

❧

All that is is the result of what we have thought.

—BUDDHA

❧

Thoughts rule the world.

—RALPH WALDO EMERSON

❧

Men imagine that thought can be kept secret, but it cannot; it rapidly crystallizes into habit, and habit solidifies into circumstance. —JAMES ALLEN

❧

Your imagination is your preview of life's coming attractions. —ALBERT EINSTEIN

❧

Thinking is the hardest work there is, which is the probable reason why so few people engage in it.

—HENRY FORD

❧

Back of every noble life there are principles that have fashioned it. —GEORGE HORACE LORIMER

❧

The mind is its own place, and in itself can make a heaven of Hell, a hell of Heaven. —JOHN MILTON

❧

You give birth to that on which you fix your mind.
——ANTOINE DE SAINT-EXUPÉRY

❧

The highest possible stage in moral culture is when we recognize that we ought to control our thoughts. ——CHARLES DARWIN

❧

Wisdom entereth not into a malicious mind.
——RABELAIS

❧

It is not enough to have a good mind. The main thing is to use it well. ——RENÉ DESCARTES

REALITY

Things are not what they seem, including us. As a Zen master put it, "How can you be happy when you spend most of your time worrying about something that doesn't even exist?" The "something" he was referring to is the ego, that confused jumble of thoughts and desires we mistake for the Self. Reality and the true perception of it lie beyond this narrow band of socially conditioned consciousness. From the perspective of Zen, to "get real" is to get out of ourselves, to release the identification with ourselves as "a thing apart." A part is in conflict with other parts; but the whole cannot be against itself. As my Zen teacher would often say: "I become the Buddha, whole universe become the Buddha."

In reality there is no better, no worse, no difference. There is no loss or gain, nothing old or new. There is nothing to compare with anything else. Everything in the universe is the one same stuff, taking on various forms or disguises. The Zen realization of "emptiness" comes with the release of the identification with, and attachment to, forms, including the physical form we call the body and the mental form we call the ego and mistake for the Self.

The deeper realization is that form *is* emptiness; emptiness, form. In other words, the spiritual reality is manifest in the physicality of the world. As Jesus said in The Gospel According to Thomas, "The Kingdom of Heaven is spread upon the earth and men do not see it."

*

In the World of Reality there is no self. There is no other-than-self. —SENG-T'SAN

*

The universe is made of one kind of whatever-it-is, which cannot be defined. —THADDEUS GOLAS

*

The universe is a single life comprising one substance and one soul.　　　——MARCUS AURELIUS

❧

It is not mind, it is not Buddha; it is not a thing.

——MA-TSU

❧

Every man takes the limits of his field of vision for the limits of the world.

——ARTHUR SCHOPENHAUER

❧

When all things are seen with equal mind, they return to their nature.　　　——SENG-T'SAN

❧

For ignorance is in reality the Buddha nature.

——CHENG-TAO KE

❧

Attachment is the greatest fabricator of illusions; reality can be attained only by someone who is detached.　　　——SIMONE WEIL

❧

O, Heart, remember thee That Man is none,
Save One.   —COVENTRY PATMORE

❧

He then learns that in going down into the secrets
of his own mind he has descended into the secrets
of all minds.   —RALPH WALDO EMERSON

❧

All that is true, by whomsoever it has been said,
has its origin in the Spirit.   —THOMAS AQUINAS

❧

If you realize what the real problem is—losing
yourself—you realize that this itself is the ultimate
trial.   —JOSEPH CAMPBELL

❧

What is reality? Selflessness.   —SUFI SAYING

❧

Love . . . is a living reality.

—ALBERT SCHWEITZER

❧

I believe that unarmed truth and unconditional love will have the final word in reality.

—MARTIN LUTHER KING, JR.

❧

Everything passes, and what remains of former times, what remains of life, is the spiritual. In everything we do, the claim of the Absolute is unchanging.

—PAUL KLEE

❧

The words of truth are always paradoxical.

—LAO-TZU

❧

All are but parts of one stupendous whole,
Whose body nature is, and God the soul.

—ALEXANDER POPE

❧

If the mind makes no discriminations, all things are as they really are.

—SENG-T'SAN

❧

God is Infinite and His Shadow is also infinite.

——MEHER BABA

❧

Compared to what we ought to be, we are half
awake. ——WILLIAM JAMES

❧

Ego-soul is the seed of birth and death,
And foolish people call it the true man.

——ZUIGAN

❧

The religious idea of God cannot do full duty for
the metaphysical infinity. ——ALAN WATTS

❧

First there is a mountain,
Then there is no mountain,
Then there is.

——ZEN SAYING

❧

A long thing is the long Body of the Buddha;
A short thing is the short Body of the Buddha.

—ZENRIN

❧

Form is emptiness, and the very emptiness is form;
emptiness does not differ from form, form does not
differ from emptiness; whatever is form, that is
emptiness, whatever is emptiness, that is form.

—HEART SUTRA

❧

Being and nonbeing create each other. —LAO-TZU

❧

I am neither God nor creature: *I am what I am, and
what I will remain,* now and forever!

—MEISTER ECKHART

❧

Do not cling to the notion of voidness, but consider
all things alike. —SARAHA

❧

Do not be idolatrous about or bound to any doctrine, theory, or ideology, even Buddhist ones. Buddhist systems of thought are guiding means; they are not absolute truth.

—VIETNAMESE BUDDHIST PRECEPT

RESPONSIBILITY

One of the great lessons of Zen is to take total responsibility for your own life. Unfortunately, many of us have been conditioned to believe, feel, and act as though the world owes us something. We complain that, as George Bernard Shaw put it, "the world will not devote itself" to making us happy. Zen says, "Why waste time and energy with regrets and whining? We have the gift of life and the opportunities of this moment."

I once asked a Zen master for his philosophy of life. In reply, he said simply, "I do not regret having been born." For me, it was a moment of illumination. When we truly celebrate and do not regret our birth, we embrace the whole of our lives. All the suffering and disappointments in life, all the imperfections in ourselves and others have come from the fact that we have been born into this world.

As the Taoists say, all things have mutually arisen. What we call the "bad" has arisen with what we call the "good"; what we call the "happy," with the "sad." Yet in truth, as the poet said, "Nothing is good or bad but thinking makes it so." When we give up the habit of making mental comparisons, we release our psychological investment in what we like and dislike and say yes to life—total and complete.

❧

All the affairs of the universe come within the range of my duty. My duties include all the affairs of the universe. The universe is my mind. My mind is the universe. —LU HSIANG-SHAN

❧

You must push yourself beyond your limits, all the time. —CARLOS CASTANEDA

❧

It is our duty as men and women to proceed as though the limits of our abilities do not exist.

—TEILHARD DE CHARDIN

❧

The difficulty in life is the choice.

—GEORGE MOORE

❧

Success on any major scale requires you to accept responsibility. . . . In the final analysis, the one quality that all successful people have . . . is the ability to take on responsibility.

—MICHAEL KORDA

❧

We didn't inherit the land from our fathers. We are borrowing it from our children.   —AMISH SAYING

❧

Therefore the considerations of the intelligent always include both benefit and harm. As they consider benefit, their work can expand; as they consider harm, their troubles can be resolved.

—SUN-TZU

❧

If a man is unhappy, remember that his unhappiness is his own fault, for God made all men to be happy . . .   —EPICTETUS

❧

Many times a day I realize how much my own outer and inner life is built upon the labors of my fellow men, both living and dead, and how earnestly I must exert myself in order to give in return as much as I have received.   —ALBERT EINSTEIN

❧

Our plans miscarry because they have no aim. When a man does not know what harbor he is making for, no wind is the right wind.   —SENECA

❧

Hold yourself responsible for a higher standard than anyone else expects of you. Never excuse yourself.
                    —HENRY WARD BEECHER

❧

Man finds the meaning of his human existence in his capacity for decision, in his freedom of choice. It is a dreadful freedom, for it also means responsibility, but without it man would be as nothing.

—WILL HERBERG

❧

You should investigate something to see its benefit or harm, examine whether it is appropriate and suitable or not; then after that you may carry it out.

—CAOTANG

❧

It is not enough to be busy, so are the ants. The question is, what are we busy about?

—HENRY DAVID THOREAU

❧

If men were Wise; the Most arbitrary Princes could not hurt them. If they are not wise, the Freest Government is compelled to be a Tyranny.

—WILLIAM BLAKE

❧

Let him who would move the world first move himself.
                                    —SENECA

❧

The great use of life is to spend it for something that will outlast it.
                                    —WILLIAM JAMES

❧

We must ask where we are and whither we are tending.
                                    —ABRAHAM LINCOLN

❧

The hardest thing to learn in life is which bridge to cross and which to burn.
                                    —DAVID RUSSELL

❧

People are always blaming their circumstances for what they are. I don't believe in circumstances. The people who get on in this world are the people who get up and look for the circumstances they want, and, if they can't find them, make them.

                    —GEORGE BERNARD SHAW

❧

The greatest griefs are those we cause ourselves.

—SOPHOCLES

❧

The greater part of all the mischief in the world arises from the fact that men do not sufficiently understand their own aims.   —JOHANN GOETHE

❧

You must be the change you wish to see in the world.   —MAHATMA GANDHI

❧

Choose always the way that seems the best, however rough it may be. Custom will soon render it easy and agreeable.   —PYTHAGORAS

❧

Self-knowledge and self-improvement are very difficult for most people. It usually needs great courage and long struggle.   —ABRAHAM MASLOW

❧

Whatever it be, every fortune is to be overcome by
bearing it.   —VIRGIL

❧

Only the individual who has come to terms with
his self can have a dispassionate attitude toward the
world.   —ERIC HOFFER

❧

Nothing happens to any man which he is not
formed by nature to bear.   —MARCUS AURELIUS

❧

Man is not the creature of circumstances. Circumstances are the creatures of men.
                              —BENJAMIN DISRAELI

❧

The injuries we do and those we suffer are seldom
weighed in the same scales.   —AESOP

❧

The violence done us by others is often less painful than that which we do to ourselves.

—DE LA ROCHEFOUCAULD

❧

Things that are done, it is needless to speak about . . . things that are past, it is needless to blame.

—CONFUCIUS

❧

Let us not underestimate the privileges of the *mediocre*. As one climbs *higher*, life becomes ever harder: the coldness increases, responsibility increases.

—FRIEDRICH NIETZSCHE

❧

To be wronged is nothing unless you continue to remember it.   —CONFUCIUS

❧

Things do not get better by being left alone.

—WINSTON CHURCHILL

❧

We have no more right to consume happiness
without producing it than to consume wealth
without producing it.   —GEORGE BERNARD SHAW

❧

This is a world of action, and not for moping and
groaning in.   —CHARLES DICKENS

BE

YOURSELF

Most Western psychological theories confuse the ego with the Self. As a result, we view the self as an object in need of adaptation or correction. On the other hand, most Eastern philosophies, including Zen, distinguish the ego from the authentic Self. The Self is to be realized, not perfected. It cannot be improved upon or in any way altered, for It remains ever transcendent to time and space and all the changes that transpire within them.

From the perspective of Zen, the ego (or mask of personality) is not to be corrected but released. The ego is the fictional social self we must lose in order to find, or realize, the authentic Self. Losing the ego does not mean despising or annihilating it but rather severing our identification with it. In the language of Zen, releasing identification with ego brings spontaneous realization of the "original" or "unborn" Self, the True or One Self in all.

Yet being yourself is more than clinging to the emptiness of spiritual Oneness. It is also participating in your becoming in the world of time and space. While we all are One in spirit, each of us is unique in nature. Being yourself means recognizing and celebrating your particular nature, your unique gifts and abilities. There is no point in trying to be somebody else or in letting concern with what other people think dictate your life. We must each find our own path and discover for ourselves the joy of being what we are.

❧

Resolve to be thyself, and know that he who finds himself, loses his misery.   —COVENTRY PATMORE

❧

If you follow your bliss, you put yourself on a kind of track, which has been there all the while waiting for you, and the life that you ought to be living is the one you are living.   —JOSEPH CAMPBELL

❧

It is the chiefest point of happiness that a man is
willing to be what he is.   —ERASMUS

❧

This above all: to thine own self be true,
And it must follow, as the night the day,
Thou canst not then be false to any man.

           —SHAKESPEARE

❧

Nothing can bring you peace but yourself.

           —RALPH WALDO EMERSON

❧

Make it thy business to know thyself, which is the
most difficult lesson in the world.

           —MIGUEL DE CERVANTES

❧

The hero's will is not that of his ancestors nor of
his society, but his own. This will to be oneself is
heroism.   —JOSÉ ORTEGA Y GASSETT

❧

The true perfection of man lies not in what man
has, but in what man is.   —OSCAR WILDE

❧

Know Thyself.   —THALES

❧

For what profit a man, if he gain the whole world
    and lose his own soul?
Or what shall a man give in exchange for his soul?
                        —MARK 8:36, 37

❧

Look within. Within is the fountain of good, and it
will ever bubble up, if thou wilt ever dig.
                        —MARCUS AURELIUS

❧

Know Ye not . . . that the spirit of God dwelleth
within you?   —I CORINTHIANS 3:16

❧

Our limited self is the wall separating us from the
self of God . . . It is being dead to self that is the
recognition of God . . .

— HAZRAT INAYAT KHAN

❧

Desires that are just are termed Truth. Without
desires, Truth cannot be understood.

— HUNG TZU-CH'ENG

❧

A musician must make his music, an artist must
paint, a poet must write if he is to ultimately be at
peace with himself.   — ABRAHAM MASLOW

❧

But do your thing and I shall know you.

— RALPH WALDO EMERSON

❧

Follow that will and that way which experience
confirms to be your own.   — CARL JUNG

❧

to be nobody-but-yourself—in a world which is
doing its best, night and day, to make you everybody else—means to fight the hardest battle which
any human being can fight; and never stop fighting.

—E. E. CUMMINGS

❧

Sooner murder an infant in its cradle than nurse
unacted desires. —WILLIAM BLAKE

❧

If I am not I, who will be?

—HENRY DAVID THOREAU

❧

To know oneself, one should assert oneself.

—ALBERT CAMUS

❧

In knowing ourselves to be unique, we possess the
capacity for becoming conscious of the infinite. But
only then! —CARL JUNG

❧

Every man has his own vocation, talent is the call.
——RALPH WALDO EMERSON

❧

If a man does not keep pace with his companions
perhaps it is because he hears a different drummer.
Let him step to the music he hears, however measured or far away.   ——HENRY DAVID THOREAU

❧

What each must seek in his life never was on land
or sea. It is something out of his own unique po-
tentiality for experience, something that never has
been and never could have been experienced by
anyone else.   ——JOSEPH CAMPBELL

❧

It is better to do your own duty, however imper-
fectly, than to assume the duties of another person,
however successfully. Prefer to die doing your own
duties: the duties of another will bring you into
great spiritual danger.   ——BHAGAVAD-GITA

❧

Thus to be independent of public opinion is the
first formal condition of achieving anything
great. . . .   —G. W. F. HEGEL

❧

NOT I—NOT ANYONE else, can travel that
road for you. You must travel it for yourself.
                              —WALT WHITMAN

❧

Whoso would be a man must be a nonconformist.
                         —RALPH WALDO EMERSON

❧

For this is the journey that men make: to find
themselves. If they fail in this, it doesn't matter
much what else they find.   —JAMES A. MICHENER

❧

When people are bored, it is primarily with their
own selves that they are bored.   —ERIC HOFFER

❧

Of all the infirmities we have, the most savage is to despise our being.　　—MICHEL DE MONTAIGNE

❧

To remain caught up in ideas and words about Zen is, as the old masters say, to "stink of Zen."

　　　　　　　　　　　　　　—ALAN WATTS

❧

The tragedy of a man's life is what dies inside of him while he lives.　　—HENRY DAVID THOREAU

❧

The only journey is the journey within.

　　　　　　　　　　—RAINER MARIA RILKE

❧

If our nature is permitted to guide our life, we grow healthy, fruitful, and happy.

　　　　　　　　　　　—ABRAHAM MASLOW

❧

Great emergencies and crises show us how much greater our vital resources are than we had supposed. —WILLIAM JAMES

❧

To hate and to fear is to be psychologically ill. It is, in fact, the consuming illness of our time.

—H. A. OVERSTREET

WORK

The Zen approach to work can be summarized in two words: *dharma* and *dō*. The term *dharma* has several meanings. As it applies to work, *dharma* means working in accord with your nature, doing what you were born to do, embracing your calling in life. The term *dō* applies to the manner and approach with which you engage your work. It means to do what you do with full attention and total commitment.

The recognition of your *dharma*, or calling in life, is not achieved by making lists of "all the things I want to do" and then mentally analyzing and sorting them out. Rather, it comes with listening to and trusting your own heart, allowing your innate compassion to guide you to the best use of your inborn talents.

It requires putting aside concepts about what you *should* do, as well as limiting beliefs about what you *could* do, and following your intuition.

The *dō*, or art, of work is a matter of bringing awareness, grace, and excellence to the way we work. The essence of art is self-forgetfulness, becoming so absorbed in, so at one with, the work that we lose all sense of "otherness." When we love what we are doing, we devote our all to it. We reach levels of concentration and absorption that transport us beyond ordinary, mundane consciousness and into the rapture of transcendence. In this way, our everyday work becomes a sacred meditation and a path to liberation.

❧

Your work is to discover your work and then with all your heart to give yourself to it.   —BUDDHA

❧

All labor that uplifts humanity has dignity and importance and should be undertaken with painstaking excellence.   —MARTIN LUTHER KING, JR.

❧

God gives every bird its food but He doesn't throw
it in the nest.   —JOSHUA HOLLAND

❧

Without work, all life goes rotten. But when work
is soulless, life stifles and dies.   —ALBERT CAMUS

❧

I was made to work. If you are equally industrious,
you will be equally successful.

—JOHANN SEBASTIAN BACH

❧

I'm a great believer in luck, and I find that the
harder I work, the more I have of it.

—THOMAS JEFFERSON

❧

Whatever is worth doing at all is worth doing well.

—PHILLIP STANHOPE

❧

If you have love you will do all things well.

—THOMAS MERTON

❧

I want to be thoroughly used up when I die, for the harder I work the more I live. I rejoice in life for its own sake. —GEORGE BERNARD SHAW

❧

The vocation, whether it be that of the farmer or the architect, is a function; the exercise of this function as regards the man himself is the most indispensable means of spiritual development, and as regards his relation to society the measure of his worth. —ANANDA K. COOMARASWAMY

❧

It is the first of all problems for a man to find out what kind of work he is to do in this universe.

—THOMAS CARLYLE

❧

Fatigue is often caused not by work, but by worry, frustration and resentment. We rarely get tired when we are doing something interesting and exciting. —DALE CARNEGIE

✍

Perfect freedom is reserved for the man who lives by his own work and in that work does what he wants to do. —R. G. COLLINGWOOD

✍

An unemployed existence is a negation worse than death itself because to live means to have something definite to do . . . a mission to fulfill . . . and in the measure in which we avoid setting our life to something, we make it empty . . . Human life, by its very nature, has to be dedicated to something.
—JOSÉ ORTEGA Y GASSET

✍

Such gardens are not made by Singing: ". . . Oh, how beautiful" and Sitting in the shade.
—RUDYARD KIPLING

✍

Everyone has been made for some particular work,
and the desire for that work has been put in every
heart.   —RUMI

❧

I think the person who takes a job in order to
live—that is to say, for the money—has turned
himself into a slave.   —JOSEPH CAMPBELL

❧

There's no substitute for hard work.

—THOMAS EDISON

❧

Make your work to be in keeping with your
purpose.   —LEONARDO DA VINCI

❧

Your motive in working should be to set others, by
your example, on the path of duty.

—BHAGAVAD-GITA

❧

The work will teach you how to do it.

—ESTONIAN PROVERB

❧

One way or another, we all have to find what best fosters the flowering of our humanity in this contemporary life, and dedicate ourselves to that.

—JOSEPH CAMPBELL

❧

Blessed is he who has found his work. Let him ask no other blessing. —THOMAS CARLYLE

❧

It is your work in life that is the ultimate seduction.

—PABLO PICASSO

❧

Wherefore by their fruits ye shall know them.

—MATTHEW 7:20

❧

If a man has important work, and enough leisure and income to enable him to do it properly, he is

in possession of as much happiness as is good for
any of the children of Adam.   —R. H. TAWNEY

❧

Work banishes those three great evils: boredom,
vice, and poverty.   —VOLTAIRE

❧

Where your talents and the needs of the world
cross, there lies your vocation.   —ARISTOTLE

❧

The decision as to what your career is to be is a
very deep and important one, and it has to do with
something like a spiritual requirement and commitment.   —JOSEPH CAMPBELL

❧

Work is the grand cure for all the maladies that
ever beset mankind—honest work which you
intend getting done.   —THOMAS CARLYLE

CREATIVITY

To live is to create. While consciously creating, we move in harmony with life, actively participating with the creative power that *is* the Universe. There is no conflict between consciously creating your life and "letting things happen." Indeed, creation is what is happening, and we are "happening" to the extent that we are consciously creating our own lives. Rather than viewing ourselves as static objects, tossed about by the waves of life, we can identify ourselves with the vast ocean of existence and consciously participate in what it is doing.

Creativity is not a special genetic endowment reserved for a favored few; neither is it the objects or events it produces. Creativity is fundamentally an attitude toward life. It requires equal parts receptivity and resourcefulness—an openness to intuitions and ideas and a readiness to put them to work. Spontaneous and disciplined, flexible and focused, the creative life is a marriage of opposites.

A creative approach to life begins with the recognition that we have all that we need, if we but know what to do with it. Nothing drains creativity like the thought that we are lacking, either in our inner or outer resources. Yet it is on precisely these kinds of thoughts that we too often dwell. The innate creativity which every human being is heir to returns to all who will give up complaining about the hand they have been dealt and learn to play the one they have.

❧

Neither a lofty degree of intelligence nor imagination nor both together go into the making of genius. Love, love, love, that is the soul of genius.

—WOLFGANG AMADEUS MOZART

❧

Imagination is the beginning of creation. You imagine what you desire; you will what you imagine, and at last you create what you will.

—GEORGE BERNARD SHAW

Think not so much of what thou hast not, as of what thou hast. —MARCUS AURELIUS

Every child is born a genius. —ALBERT EINSTEIN

Towering genius disdains a beaten path. It seeks regions hitherto unexplored. —ABRAHAM LINCOLN

The great creative individual . . . is capable of more wisdom and virtue than collective man ever can be. —JOHN STUART MILL

If you see in any given situation only what everybody else can see, you can be said to be so much a
representative of your culture that you are a victim
of it.   —S. I. HAYAKAWA

❧

A crank is a man with a new idea—until it catches
on.   —MARK TWAIN

❧

Men must find and feel and represent in all of their
creative works Man the Eternal, the creator.

—TAGORE

❧

You see things and say, "why?" but I dream things
that never were and say, "why not?"

—GEORGE BERNARD SHAW

❧

To be willing to suffer in order to create is one
thing; to realize that one's creation necessitates
one's suffering, that suffering is one of the greatest
of God's gifts, is almost to reach a mystical solution
to the problem of evil.   —J. W. SULLIVAN

❧

Creative minds always have been known to survive any kind of bad training.　　—ANNA FREUD

❧

Without this playing with fantasy no creative work has ever yet come to birth. The debt we owe to the play of the imagination is incalculable.

　　　　　　　　　　　　—CARL JUNG

❧

To be properly expressed a thing must proceed from within, moved by its form.

　　　　　　　　　　　　—MEISTER ECKHART

❧

The real object of education is to have a man in the condition of continually asking questions.

　　　　　　　　—BISHOP MANDELL CREIGHTON

❧

If we want to make something really superb of this planet, there is nothing whatever that can stop us.

　　　　　　　　　　　—SHEPHERD MEAD

❧

No matter how old you get, if you keep the desire
to be creative, you're keeping the man-child alive.

—JOHN CASSAVETES

❧

As a rule, indeed, grown-up people are fairly
correct on matters of fact; it is in the higher gift of
imagination that they are so sadly to seek.

—KENNETH GRAHAME

❧

All life is an experiment.

—OLIVER WENDELL HOLMES

❧

It is the lone worker who makes the first advance
in a subject: the details may be worked out by a
team, but the prime idea is due to the enterprise,
thought and perception of an individual.

—SIR ALEXANDER FLEMING

❧

It isn't that they can't see the solution. It is that they can't see the problem.   —G. K. CHESTERTON

❧

In creating, the only hard thing's to begin.
                              —JAMES RUSSELL LOWELL

❧

Discovery consists in seeing what everybody else has seen and thinking what nobody else has thought.   —ALBERT SZENT-GYÖRGYI

HUMOR

Like a sudden a bolt of lightning, a shot of humor can pierce the veil of automatic mundane consciousness and charge the moment with insight and energy. Laughter lifts our spirits and restores our vitality. Humor is often the result of looking at painful situations from a place of detachment. Since, as the Buddha tells us, life *is* suffering, there are plenty of opportunities for humor.

We suffer because we lose. We lose respect and companions; we lose possessions and titles; we lose health and wealth; and ultimately, we lose life itself. Grief is the feeling associated with loss. Originally, our word *grief* meant "heavy." If we are not careful, *we* can become heavy, weighed down, or "depressed," by the grief that attends every life. More than anything, grief has the capacity to separate or unite us. Humor lifts us above the isolation of our individual grief and reminds us that pain is something we share with all sentient beings.

Zen invites us in on the cosmic joke of existence, reminding us how silly we are to seek permanence in impermanence, how foolish to seek in the outside world that which resides within. In so doing, it helps us to keep a perspective on our personal dramas and not take them too seriously. If, as someone once said in jest, the best cure for hypochondria is to become interested in someone else's body, then the best cure for self-important stuffiness is to see ourselves as others see us. We are all a little ridiculous—and all the more so when we forget it.

❧

We should tackle reality in a slightly joking way . . . otherwise we miss its point. —LAWRENCE DURRELL

❧

When a man is wrapped up in himself, he makes a pretty small package.　　　　　　—JOHN RUSKIN

❧

A man isn't poor if he can still laugh.

—RAYMOND HITCHCOCK

❧

Laughter is the jam on the toast of life. It adds flavor, keeps it from being too dry, and makes it easier to swallow.

—DIANE JOHNSON

❧

Comedy is the last refuge of the nonconformist.

—GILBERT SELEES

❧

We must laugh at man to avoid crying for him.

—NAPOLÉON BONAPARTE

❧

Why wait for Heaven? Have fun now. . . . Let's choose to be like the angels who fly freely because they take themselves lightly.

—RUTH HANNA

❧

Sometimes I think that God in creating man some-
what overestimated his ability.   —OSCAR WILDE

❧

He deserves paradise who can make his companions
laugh.   —THE KORAN

❧

Our sincerest laughter
With some pain is fraught.
        —SHELLEY

❧

Every man is important if he loses his life; and
every man is funny if he loses his hat and has to
run after it.   —G. K. CHESTERTON

❧

Laughter is the shortest distance between two
people.   —VICTOR BORGE

✄

If you wish to glimpse inside a human soul and get
to know a man . . . just watch him laugh. If he
laughs well, he's a good man.

—FYODOR DOSTOYEVSKY

✄

The love of truth lies at the root of much humor.

—ROBERTSON DAVIES

✄

A person without a sense of humor is like a wagon
without springs—jolted by every pebble in the
road. —HENRY WARD BEECHER

✄

The Way is really rather exasperating.

—R. H. BLYTH

✄

Men show their character in nothing more clearly
than by what they think laughable.

—JOHANN GOETHE

❧

People who do not know how to laugh are always pompous and self-conceited.

—WILLIAM THACKERAY

❧

You grow up the day you can have your first real laugh—at yourself. —ETHEL BARRYMORE

❧

Life does not cease to be funny when people die any more than it ceases to be serious when people laugh. —GEORGE BERNARD SHAW

❧

Laugh at yourself first, before anyone else can.

—ELSA MAXWELL

❧

The whole world is a comedy for those who think, a tragedy for those who feel.

—HORACE WALPOLE

❧

The burden of the self is lightened when I laugh at myself. —TAGORE

❧

I have often been asked what I thought was the secret of Buddha's smile. It is—it can only be— that he smiles at himself for searching all those years for what he already possessed.

—PAUL BRUNTON

SELF-CONFIDENCE

Genuine self-confidence is not a matter of a puffed-up ego asserting superiority. Rather, it is recognizing the intrinsic worth of all human beings, including yourself. Respect the dignity and inherent worth of all human beings, regardless of their station in life or outer accomplishments, and you will respect yourself. Recognize the resourcefulness, creativity, and ability inherent in all human beings, and you can't help but value your own gifts and abilities.

The opposite of self-confidence is not insecurity or inadequacy but self-consciousness. Feelings of insecurity and inadequacy are only symptoms, the inevitable result of self-conscious thinking. Stop the mental chatter and your natural self-confidence returns. This is where meditation and the Zen notion of single-mindedness come into play (for more on meditation, see page 164). Single-mindedness means simply doing what we are doing, without daydreaming, on the one hand, or self-consciously observing ourselves, on the other.

Nothing destroys self-confidence like being selfish and petty. Perhaps the greatest boost to self-confidence is the embrace of a larger-than-self purpose. Instead of worrying about how we are being perceived or judged by others, we can devote ourselves to important work—without assuming self-importance or pretentiousness. Again, self-confidence is nothing special. It is the absence of self-consciousness, nothing more, nothing less.

❧

The point we emphasize is strong confidence in our original nature. —SHUNRYU SUZUKI

❧

They conquer who believe they can.

—RALPH WALDO EMERSON

❧

Always bear in mind that your own resolution to succeed is more important than any other one thing. —ABRAHAM LINCOLN

❧

To believe that what has not occurred in history will not occur at all, is to argue disbelief in the dignity of man. —MAHATMA GANDHI

❧

I have learned this at least by my experiment: that if one advances confidently in the direction of his dreams, and endeavors to live the life which he has imagined, he will meet with a success unexpected in common hours. —HENRY DAVID THOREAU

❧

Man is what he believes. —ANTON CHEKHOV

❧

The beginning is the most important part of the work. —PLATO

❧

Go to the battlefield firmly confident of victory and you come home with no wounds whatsoever.

——UESUGI KENSHIN

❧

Every individual has a place to fill in the world and is important in some respect, whether he chooses to be so or not. ——NATHANIEL HAWTHORNE

❧

No one can make you feel inferior without your consent. ——ELEANOR ROOSEVELT

❧

Self-esteem is the reputation we acquire with ourselves. ——NATHANIEL BRANDEN

❧

Nothing splendid has ever been achieved except by those who dared believe that something inside them was superior to circumstance. ——JOHN BARTON

❧

They can because they think they can.   —VIRGIL

❧

Ask and it shall be given unto you. Seek and ye
shall find.   —LUKE 11:9

❧

Speak the affirmative; emphasize your choice by
utterly ignoring all that you reject.
                    —RALPH WALDO EMERSON

❧

He who hesitates is lost.   —ENGLISH PROVERB

❧

So long as a man imagines that he cannot do this
or that, so long is he determined not to do it.
                        —BENEDICT SPINOZA

❧

All things are possible until they are proved
impossible—and even the impossible may be only
so as of now.   —PEARL S. BUCK

❧

To the degree that we become enemies to the highest and best within us, do we become enemies to all. —RALPH W. TRINE

❧

The future belongs to those who believe in the beauty of their dreams. —ELEANOR ROOSEVELT

❧

The greatest achievement was at first and for a time a dream. —JAMES ALLEN

❧

When you are inspired by some great purpose, some extraordinary project, all your thoughts break their bounds: Your mind transcends limitations, your consciousness expands in every direction and you find yourself in a new, great and wonderful world. Dormant forces, faculties and talents become alive, and you discover yourself to be a greater person by far than you ever dreamed yourself to be.

—PATANJALI

❧

Whether you think you can or you can't—you are
right.   —HENRY FORD

❧

In the long run you hit only what you aim at.
Therefore, though you should fail immediately, you
had better aim at something high.

—HENRY DAVID THOREAU

COMPASSION

Compassion is not sentimentality. It is not about being nice, polite, or pleasing. Indeed, compassion may often take on a wrathful form or manifest itself in a tough love. There can be no compassion (*karunā*) without wisdom (*prajñā*) and no true wisdom without compassion.

Genuine compassion arises with the realization of identity. When we experience the sufferings of others as our own and respond in love, we are acting from compassion. Compassionate acts come in all shapes and sizes. It's not the size or scope of the action but the motive that counts.

From the Buddhist perspective, compassion ultimately generates the desire to liberate others from *samsara,* the cycle of rebirth. This supreme compassion is exemplified in the bodhisattva, who, having gained his or her own release, postpones it for the sake of freeing others. Like one who has escaped a burning building and returns to help save those still trapped in the flames, the compassionate bodhisattva seeks not her own safety but the release of all sentient beings.

❧

Can I see another's woe
And not be in sorrow too?
Can I see another's grief
And not seek for kind relief?

——WILLIAM BLAKE

❧

The good man is the friend of all living things.

——MAHATMA GANDHI

❧

There is a comfort in the strength of love;
'Twill make a thing endurable, which else
Would overset the brain, or break the heart.

——WILLIAM WORDSWORTH

❧

Love is love's reward.   —JOHN DRYDEN

❧

What thou lovest well remains, the rest is dross
What thou lov'st well shall not be reft from thee
What thou lov'st well is thy true heritage.
                              —EZRA POUND

❧

He who wants to do good knocks at the gate; he
who loves finds the gate open.   —TAGORE

❧

I cry: Love! Love! Love! happy happy Love! free
as the mountain wind!   —WILLIAM BLAKE

❧

My life is an indivisible whole, and all my activities
run into one another; and they have their rise in
my insatiable love of mankind.

                              —MAHATMA GANDHI

❧

Have we not come to such an impasse in the
modern world that we must love our enemies—or
else? The chain reaction of evil—hate begetting
hate, wars producing more wars—must be broken,
or else we shall be plunged into the dark abyss
of annihilation.   —MARTIN LUTHER KING, JR.

❧

The only lasting beauty is the beauty of the heart.
                                                    —RUMI

❧

I feel the capacity to care is the thing which gives
life its deepest significance and meaning.
                                          —PABLO CASALS

❧

Love until it hurts. Real love is always painful and
hurts: then it is real and pure.   —MOTHER TERESA

❧

No one must shut his eyes and regard as non-existent the sufferings of which he spares himself the sight. Let no one regard as light the burden of his responsibility. —ALBERT SCHWEITZER

To love is to transform; to be a poet.
—NORMAN O. BROWN

I hold myself to be incapable of hating any being on earth. By a long course of prayerful discipline, I have ceased for over forty years to hate anybody. I know this is a big claim. Nevertheless, I make it in all humility. —MAHATMA GANDHI

One learns through the heart, not the eyes or the intellect. —MARK TWAIN

Without love the acquisition of knowledge only increases confusion and leads to self-destruction.
—J. KRISHNAMURTI

❧

Today . . . we know that all living beings who strive to maintain life and who long to be spared pain—all living beings on earth are our neighbors.

—ALBERT SCHWEITZER

❧

The best portion of a good man's life—his little, nameless, unremembered acts of kindness and of love.   —WILLIAM WORDSWORTH

❧

Joyously participate in the sorrows of others.

—BUDDHA

❧

Come out of the circle of time, and into the circle of love.   —RUMI

❧

The heart has its reasons that the mind knows nothing of.   —BLAISE PASCAL

❧

To love and to be loved is the greatest happiness.

—SYDNEY SMITH

❧

Love, and do as you please.   —THOMAS AQUINAS

❧

Many waters cannot quench love, neither can the floods drown it.   —SONG OF SOLOMON 8:7

❧

Love conquers all things; let us too surrender to Love.   —VIRGIL

❧

The Spirit of Buddha is that of great loving kindness and compassion.   —BUDDHA

❧

He that dwelleth in love dwelleth in God, and God in him.   —I JOHN 4:16

❧

We are all born for love. . . . It is the principle of existence and its only end.

—BENJAMIN DISRAELI

❧

Take away love and our earth is a tomb.

—ROBERT BROWNING

❧

Virtue is to love men.   —CONFUCIUS

❧

The highest wisdom is loving kindness.

—THE TALMUD

❧

Accustomed long to contemplating Love and
    Compassion,
I have forgotten all difference
between myself and others.

—MILAREPA

❧

All the world is full of suffering, it is also full of
overcoming it. —HELEN KELLER

🌿

Every atom belonging to me as good belongs to
you. —WALT WHITMAN

🌿

Love is patient; love is kind and envies no one . . .
There is nothing love cannot face; there is no limit
to its faith, hope, and its endurance. Love will
never come to an end. —I CORINTHIANS 13:4–8

🌿

You want to be loved because you do not love;
but the moment you love, it is finished, you are
no longer inquiring whether or not somebody loves
you. —J. KRISHNAMURTI

JOY

Joy, or in Buddhist terms, *ānanda* (bliss), is our natural state. It is not something that we achieve or win, find or acquire. In fact, the irony of happiness is that the more we chase it, the more it flees us. The enduring joy is the one inherent in our being. It is not to be found in a person, condition, or object. It is part and parcel of the consciousness of life. To the extent that we live in consciousness, we live in joy. To the extent that we are unconscious, we miss the bliss.

Starting from the recognition that we are complete, we experience a bliss transcendent to pleasure and pain. Beyond the ups and downs, the inevitable turns of fortune, we embrace the whole of our lives in gratitude. Dostoyevsky called man "the ungrateful biped." Unfortunately, this is often the case, but he also said: "Man is unhappy because he doesn't realize he's happy . . . If anyone finds out, he'll become happy at once."

In Zen, there is a practice of awareness referred to as "inhibiting the inhibition," or "blocking the block." If, as all the enlightened masters have said, true joy is our natural state of being, then we needn't do anything to acquire it. Rather, we have only to become aware of how we are blocking it by insisting on the fulfillment of some condition before we can be happy. This awareness itself blocks the block and returns us to our natural state of bliss.

❦

What a wonderful life I've had! I only wish I'd realized it sooner.　　　　　　　　　　—COLLETTE

❦

Look at everything as though you were seeing it for the first or last time. Then your time on earth will be filled with glory. . . .　　　—BETTY SMITH

❧

Scatter Joy.   —RALPH WALDO EMERSON

❧

The pursuit of happiness is a most ridiculous
phrase: If you pursue happiness you'll never find it.
                                        —C. P. SNOW

❧

The happiness of your life depends on the quality
of your thoughts.   —MARCUS AURELIUS

❧

This is the true joy in life, the being used for a
purpose recognized by yourself as a mighty one.
                            —GEORGE BERNARD SHAW

❧

Perfect happiness is the absence of striving for happiness.   —CHUANG-TSE

❧

Take thy Bliss O Man!   —WILLIAM BLAKE

❧

A joyful heart is the inevitable result of a heart
burning with love.   ——MOTHER TERESA

❧

Happiness is a perfume you cannot pour on others
without getting a few drops on yourself.
                    ——RALPH WALDO EMERSON

❧

All that we behold is full of blessings.
                    ——WILLIAM WORDSWORTH

❧

Many persons have a wrong idea of what consti-
tutes true happiness. It is not attained through self-
gratification, but through fidelity to a purpose.
                    ——HELEN KELLER

❧

Very little is needed to make a happy life. It is all
within yourself, in your way of thinking.
                    ——MARCUS AURELIUS

❧

The way to be happy is to make others so.

—ROBERT INGERSOLL

❧

I love laughing. —WILLIAM BLAKE

❧

The miracle is not that we do this work, but that
we are happy to do it. —MOTHER TERESA

❧

The happiest man is he who learns from nature the
lesson of worship. —RALPH WALDO EMERSON

❧

Ask yourself whether you are happy, and you cease
to be so. —JOHN STUART MILL

❧

Happiness doesn't depend on what we have, but it does depend on how we feel towards what we have. We can be happy with little and miserable with much. —W. D. HOARD

✱

One joy scatters a hundred griefs.
—CHINESE PROVERB

✱

One should sympathize with the joy, the beauty, the color of life—the less said about life's sores the better. —OSCAR WILDE

✱

Let no one who loves be called altogether unhappy. Even love unreturned has its rainbow.
—JAMES M. BARRIE

✱

A merry heart doeth good like a medicine; but a broken spirit drieth the bones. —PROVERBS 17:2

✱

To enjoy—to love a thing for its own sake and for
no other reason.   —LEONARDO DA VINCI

❧

The sense of living is joy enough.
                    —EMILY DICKINSON

❧

If I keep a green bough in my heart, the singing
bird will come.   —CHINESE PROVERB

❧

The greatest happiness you can have is knowing
that you do not necessarily require happiness.
                    —WILLIAM SAROYAN

❧

Within your own house dwells the treasure of joy;
so why do you go begging from door to door?
                    —SUFI SAYING

❧

Joy is not in things; it is in us.

——CHARLES WAGNER

❧

Cheerfulness is as natural to the heart of a man in strong health as color is to his cheeks.

——JOHN RUSKIN

❧

We shall never know all the good that a simple smile can do. ——MOTHER TERESA

"What is Zen?" In reply, Chao-Chou said to the monk, "Have you finished your rice? Then go wash your bowl!" Discipline is simply a matter of doing what we must, without wasting time or energy worrying about whether or not we feel like it. When we develop the habit of plunging in without whining, complaining, or procrastinating, we are on our way to genuine freedom.

We may not want to face it in such stark terms, but the choice is self-discipline or dependency; boss yourself or be bossed. We require a boss because we lack the discipline to boss ourselves. We resent the boss because he or she reminds us of our dependency. Resentment, in turn, robs us of the creative power we need to break the yoke of dependency. As we break through the comfort zones of limited thinking and habitual behavior, we discover that freedom is not the ability to do what we feel like doing but the ability to choose what to do and follow through.

Discipline is enlightened tenacity. Wisdom separates discipline from stubborn pride or obsessive compulsion. Too often we waste our fight. We squander the vital energy that could be channeled into creative discipline on vain and neurotic attempts to protect our egos. Then we wonder why we lack discipline. If we will but listen, the wisdom of the heart will tell us what is worth fighting for and what isn't. Then it is simply a matter of mustering the courage and tenacity to stay the course.

❧

Choose always the way that seems the best,
however rough it may be, custom will soon render
it easy and agreeable.   —PYTHAGORAS

❧

He only is happy as well as great who needs
neither to obey nor command in order to be something.   —JOHANN GOETHE

❧

He who cannot obey himself will be commanded.
This is the nature of living creatures.

—FRIEDRICH NIETZSCHE

❧

Wisdom begins with sacrifice of immediate pleasures for long-range purposes.

—LOUIS FINKELSTEIN

❧

Let us train our minds to desire what the situation
demands. —SENECA

❧

Nothing exterior shall ever take command of me.

—WALT WHITMAN

❧

The disciplined man masters thoughts by stillness
and emotions by calmness. —LAO-TZU

❧

In all human affairs there are efforts, and there are results, and the strength of the effort is the measure of the result.   —JAMES ALLEN

❧

It is one thing to praise discipline, and another thing to submit to it.   —MIGUEL DE CERVANTES

❧

Carpenters bend wood; fletchers bend arrows; wise men fashion themselves.   —BUDDHA

❧

Strength doesn't come from physical capacity. It comes from indomitable will.

—MAHATMA GANDHI

❧

Discipline divorced from wisdom is not true discipline, but merely the meaningless following of custom, which is a disguise for ignorance.

—TAGORE

&

We go all wrong by too strenuous a resolution to go all right. —NATHANIEL HAWTHORNE

&

No man is free who cannot command himself.

—PYTHAGORAS

&

Perhaps the most valuable result of all education is the ability to make yourself do the thing you have to do, when it ought to be done, whether you like it or not. —THOMAS HUXLEY

&

There never has been, and cannot be, a good life without self-control. —LEO TOLSTOY

&

What is freedom? It means not being slave to any circumstance, to any restraint, to any chance.

—SENECA

❧

Men's natures are alike; it is their habits that separate them. —CONFUCIUS

❧

The roots of education are bitter, but the fruit is
sweet. —ARISTOTLE

❧

He who would accomplish little must sacrifice little;
he who would achieve much must sacrifice much;
he who would attain highly must sacrifice greatly.
—JAMES ALLEN

❧

Put all your eggs in one basket and—watch that
basket. —MARK TWAIN

❧

It is easier to go down a hill than up, but the view
is from the top. —ARNOLD BENNETT

❧

Discipline is learnt in the school of adversity.

—MAHATMA GANDHI

⚘

Most men make use of the first part of their life to render the last part miserable.

—JEAN DE LA BRUYÈRE

⚘

Everybody, soon or late, sits down to a banquet of consequences.　—ROBERT LOUIS STEVENSON

⚘

If people knew how hard I worked to get my mastery, it wouldn't seem so wonderful after all.

—MICHELANGELO

⚘

Do not pray for easy lives. Pray to be stronger men! Do not pray for tasks equal to your powers. Pray for powers equal to your tasks.

—PHILLIPS BROOKS

⚘

Practice is the best of all instructions.

—ARISTOTLE

❧

Good is best when soonest wrought. . . .

—ROBERT SOUTHWELL

❧

No man is more miserable than he that hath no adversity.   —JEREMY TAYLOR

❧

Conquer thyself. Till thou hast done this, thou art a slave.   —RICHARD F. BURTON

❧

He who would arrive at the appointed end must follow a single road and not wander through many ways.   —SENECA

WONDER

Life is a marvel and a mystery. To watch a sunset or
the play of light on a leaf, to experience the taste of
our food or the movements of our bodies is to be in
the presence of a mystery. Yet most of us have become so numb that we miss what is happening around
and within us. The simple joys of life elude us. We
require tremendous stimulation to feel any aliveness
or excitement. Yet when this noise has subsided, we
are even duller than before.

Every child is full of simple wonder. How have
we become so numb? Part of this numbing is the
result of having shut down from past psychological
pain, and part is a function of the culture in which

we live. In our efforts to protect ourselves from physical and emotional pain, we shut down to life and shut out the wonder of it. We cannot dull ourselves to the pains of life without at the same time dulling ourselves to its simple pleasures.

Today we are bombarded with more information than we can possibly process. We often must fit ourselves into someone else's schedule and are constantly rushing about, without taking the time to really experience our own bodies or life around us. Beyond this, we have accepted a cultural convention that to act "grown up" and mature is to act jaded and cynical. How marvelous to return to the simplicity of the child, to once again see and appreciate the joys and mysteries of this life. The wonder is all around us.

❧

I do not know what I may appear to the world; but to myself I seem to have been only like a boy playing on the seashore, and diverting myself in now and then finding a smoother pebble or a prettier shell than the ordinary, whilst the great ocean of truth lay all undiscovered before me.

—ISAAC NEWTON

❧

Life is a series of surprises.

—RALPH WALDO EMERSON

❧

Never say there is nothing beautiful in the world anymore. There is always something to make you wonder, in the shape of a leaf, the trembling of a tree. —ALBERT SCHWEITZER

❧

The most beautiful thing we can experience is the mysterious. It is the source of all true art and all science. He to whom this emotion is a stranger, who can no longer pause to wonder and stand rapt in awe, is as good as dead: his eyes are closed.

—ALBERT EINSTEIN

❧

If all men lead mechanical, unpoetical lives, this is the real nihilism, the real undoing of the world.

—R. H. BLYTH

❧

Numberless are the world's wonders, but none more
wonderful than man. —SOPHOCLES

❧

Look, children, hailstones!
Let's rush out!
—BASHŌ

❧

All of life is an experiment. The more experiments
you make the better. —RALPH WALDO EMERSON

❧

The longer I live, the more beautiful life becomes.
—FRANK L. WRIGHT

❧

The mystery of life is not a problem to be solved,
it is a reality to be lived.
—VAN DER LEEUWARDEN

❧

If there is a sin against life, it consists perhaps not
so much in despairing of life as in hoping for
another life and in eluding the implaccable grandeur
of this life.   —ALBERT CAMUS

❦

Nothing is more simple than greatness. Indeed, to
be simple is to be great.

—RALPH WALDO EMERSON

❦

The Tao's principle is spontaneity.   —LAO-TZU

THE

GAME
OF

LIFE

So often in our struggle for recognition and results, we forget that life is a game to be played. Zen tells us that getting caught up in the cravings of the ego breeds tension, anxiety, and resentment, turning this wonderful play of life into a deadly serious affair. Most of all, the ego craves attention. It wants to be thought of as special and enviable. Freeing ourselves from the feelings of dependency and resentment that result from seeking the approval of others or from defending ourselves against their ridicule restores a youthful innocence and exuberance to life. Playing the game of life with buoyancy and zest requires the release of attachment to externals—to people, places, things, or events as the source of our happiness.

We find it easier to concentrate on what we are doing when we are no longer using our actions to solve our psychological problems or to fulfill unmet needs for love and approval that we have carried since childhood. We can play the game of society or career without believing that "success," or the social approval and status it brings, make us any better as human beings—or that we are any worse for failing to achieve these. The irony is that the more we feel we need to win, the less likely we are to, or to enjoy it, if we do. When we do what we do for its own sake, it remains play. When we love and enjoy what we are doing, we do it well—naturally.

❧

Not to be bound by rules, but to be creating one's own rules—this is the kind of life which Zen is trying to have us live.   —D. T. SUZUKI

❧

If you follow all the rules, you miss all the fun.
                         —KATHARINE HEPBURN

❧

The trouble with the rat race is that even if you
win you're still a rat.   —LILY TOMLIN

❧

The game is not about becoming somebody; it's
about becoming nobody.   —RAM DASS

❧

All the world's a stage,
And all the men and women merely players.
                              —SHAKESPEARE

❧

The beater and the beaten: Mere players of a game
ephemeral as a dream.   —MUSO

❧

This then, is the human problem; there is a price to
be paid for every increase in consciousness. We
cannot be more sensitive to pleasure without being
more sensitive to pain.   —ALAN WATTS

❧

Everybody lives by selling something.
—ROBERT LOUIS STEVENSON

❧

The only difference between a wise man and a fool
is that the wise man knows he's playing.
—FRITZ PERLS

❧

Human affairs are like a chess game: Only those
who do not take it seriously can be called good
players. —HUNG TZU-CH'ENG

❧

Life must be lived as play. —PLATO

❧

The importance and unimportance of the self
cannot be exaggerated. —R. H. BLYTH

❧

For wayfarers of all times, the right strategy for
skillfully spreading the Way lies in adapting to

communicate. Those who do not know how to adapt stick to the letter and cling to doctrines, get stuck on forms and mired in sentiments—none of them succeed in strategic adaptation.

—ZHANTANG

✿

Zen is the game of insight, the game of discovering who you are beneath the social masks.

—R. H. BLYTH

✿

By honors, medals, titles no true man is elevated. To realize that which we are, this is the honor for which we are created.　　　—ANGELUS SILESIUS

✿

The play's the thing.　　　—SHAKESPEARE

✿

Economics and politics are the governing powers of life today, and that's why everything is screwy.

—JOSEPH CAMPBELL

❧

The world is his who can see through its preten-
sion. What deafness, what stone-blind custom, what
overgrown error you behold, is there only by
sufference—your sufference. See it to be a lie, and
you have already dealt it its mortal blow.

—RALPH WALDO EMERSON

❧

Many do not know that we are here in this world
to live in harmony. —BUDDHA

❧

The life of Zen begins, therefore, in a disillusion
with the pursuit of goals which do not really
exist—the good without the bad, the gratification of
a self which is no more than an idea, and the
morrow which never comes. —ALAN WATTS

❧

Is the system going to flatten you out and deny
you your humanity, or are you going to be able to
make use of the system to the attainment of human
purposes? —JOSEPH CAMPBELL

INTEGRITY

While today we think of integrity in terms of adherence to ethical standards, in its original sense, the word meant simply "wholeness." Integrity isn't a matter of molding ourselves to fit abstract moral concepts of what we should be or do, but of responding to life in a natural and authentic way. It is this intuitive, preconscious, spontaneous naturalness that Zen celebrates as an essential characteristic of the true man or woman.

The Cha'n, or Zen, tradition developed in China as a kind of fusion between Indian Buddhism and Chinese Taoism. From the Taoist perspective, what is good is what is intuitive and natural. Codes of ethics and moral standards to live by are not demonstrations of integrity but evidence that it has already been lost. When we have lost touch with our genuine integrity and no longer trust our natural or basic goodness, we resort to concepts of right and wrong, good and bad. Those who get caught up in moral judgments try to impose their ideas of right and wrong on others. Interpersonal conflict and, ultimately, wars and great human suffering are the inevitable result.

When our hearts are open, we are in touch with a profound intuitive intelligence, which the Buddhists call *prajñā*, or the "wisdom of the heart." When we learn to listen to and trust this intelligence, we have no need for mental concepts of right and wrong. Trust your heart and you will not stray far from the path of life.

❧

The goody-goodies are the thieves of virtue.

—CONFUCIUS

❧

"Honesty is the best policy," but he who acts on that principle is not an honest man.

—RICHARD WHATELY

❧

Be not simply good—be good for something.
—HENRY DAVID THOREAU

❧

You judge a person like you judge an apple tree,
by the fruit it produces. —ABRAHAM MASLOW

❧

Conform and be dull. —JAMES FRANK DOBIE

❧

If someone tells you he's going to make a "realistic
decision," you immediately understand that he's resolved to do something bad. —MARY MCCARTHY

❧

It's motive alone that gives character to the actions
of men. —JEAN DE LA BRUYÈRE

❧

Think nothing profitable to you which compels you
to break a promise, to lose your self-respect, to

hate any person, to suspect, to curse, to act the hypocrite, to desire anything that needs walls and curtains about it. —MARCUS AURELIUS

𝕤

The superior man understands what is right; the inferior understands what will sell. —CONFUCIUS

𝕤

People should respect public opinion in so far as it is necessary to avoid starvation and to keep out of prison, but anything that goes beyond this is voluntary submission to an unnecessary tyranny.

—BERTRAND RUSSELL

𝕤

There is only one way to achieve happiness on this
   terrestrial ball,
And that is to have either a clear conscience, or none
   at all. —OGDEN NASH

𝕤

One is always seeking the touchstone that will dissolve one's deficiencies as a person and as a craftsman. And one is always bumping up against the

fact that there is none except hard work, concentration, and continued application.

—PAUL WILLIAM GALLICO

❧

Conformity is the jailer of freedom and the enemy
of growth.　　　　　　　—JOHN F. KENNEDY

❧

Moral courage and character go hand in hand . . . a
man of real character is consistently courageous,
being imbued with a basic integrity and a firm
sense of principle.　　　　　　—MARTHA BOAZ

❧

Undertake not what you can not perform, but be
careful to keep your promises.

—GEORGE WASHINGTON

❧

We always know that society is full of folly and
will deceive us in the matter of humanity. It is an
unreliable horse, and blind into the bargain. Woe to
the driver if he falls asleep.

—ALBERT SCHWEITZER

133

✿

Rest satisfied with doing well, and leave others to talk of you as they will. —PYTHAGORAS

✿

Live as you will have wished to have lived when you are dying. —CHRISTIAN GELLERT

✿

Public opinion is a weak tyrant compared with our own private opinion. What a man thinks of himself, that is what determines, or rather, indicates, his fate. —HENRY DAVID THOREAU

✿

A man has to live with himself, and he should see to it that he always has good company.

—CHARLES EVANS HUGHES

✿

Do not seek for the truth, only stop having an opinion. —SENG-T'SAN

❧

Don't bother just to be better than your contemporaries or your predecessors. Try to be better than yourself.   —WILLIAM FAULKNER

❧

To be a warrior is to learn to be genuine in every moment of your life.   —CHÖGYAM TRUNGPA

❧

The only real valuable thing is intuition.
                              —ALBERT EINSTEIN

❧

Don't listen to what they say. Go see.
                              —CHINESE PROVERB

❧

So our self-feeling in this world depends entirely on what we back ourselves to be and do.
                              —WILLIAM JAMES

❧

The easiest person to deceive is one's ownself.

—EDWARD BULWER-LYTTON

❧

While it is true that an inherently free and scrupu-
lous individual may be destroyed, such an individual can never be enslaved or used as a blind tool.

—ALBERT EINSTEIN

❧

Don't listen to friends when the Friend inside you
says, "Do this." —MAHATMA GANDHI

❧

There comes a time when one must take a position
that is neither safe, nor politic, nor popular, but he
must take it because his conscience tells him it is
right . . . —MARTIN LUTHER

SELFLESS

SERVICE

Selfless service is the spirit of compassion in action. It has nothing to do with trying to accumulate good karma, impressing others, or puffing up our egos with how good or generous we are. It is a natural result of being true to who and what we are, responding to the innate spontaneous impulse to spread joy and eliminate suffering in the lives of others. It has been said that one selfless act destroys ten thousand *sanskaras* (the subtle impressions that are the root and record of karma).

In any moment, any of us, moved by our native compassion, may respond with selfless action. Yet a life dedicated to service to our fellow beings can only arise from the ashes of the ego. When, once and for all, we have seen the vanity and futility of ego-based desires, when we admit we have nothing to protect, when we give up trying to acquire and hold, we realize there is nothing to do. Only then can we find the true beauty, the genuine poetry in life that gives rise to selfless service. Thoreau said: "The art of life, of a poet's life, is, not having anything to do, to do something." The "something" to do is to serve humankind.

❧

From ancient times . . . the true practicer of Buddhism has been poor, endured physical hardships, and wasted nothing. He has been motivated by compassion and the Way.　　　—DŌGEN

❧

Get beyond love and grief; exist for the good of man.　　　—HA GAKURE

❧

Only a life lived for others is a life worthwhile.

　　　—ALBERT EINSTEIN

❧

In nothing do men approach so nearly to the gods
as in doing good to men.   ——CICERO

❦

I don't know what your destiny will be, but one
thing I know: the only ones among you who will
be really happy are those who have sought and
found how to serve.   ——ALBERT SCHWEITZER

❦

How can I be useful, of what service can I be?
There is something inside me, what can it be?
                              ——VINCENT VAN GOGH

❦

The sole meaning of life is to serve humanity.
                              ——LEO TOLSTOY

❦

Maturing adults . . . would want . . . each on his
own or in fellowship with others, to undertake
some project for human betterment.
                              ——H. A. OVERSTREET

❧

A person starts to live when he can live outside of himself.
— ALBERT EINSTEIN

❧

We begin from the recognition that all beings cherish happiness and do not want suffering. It then becomes both morally wrong and pragmatically unwise to pursue only one's own happiness oblivious to the feelings and aspirations of all others who surround us as members of the same human family. The wiser course is to think of others when pursuing our own happiness.
— TENZIN GYATSO (*The 14th Dalai Lama*)

❧

The most sublime act is to set another before you.
— WILLIAM BLAKE

❧

When we quit thinking primarily about ourselves and our own self-preservation, we undergo a truly heroic transformation of consciousness.
— JOSEPH CAMPBELL

❧

You ask me for a motto. Here it is: SERVICE.

—ALBERT SCHWEITZER

❧

When your thinking rises above concern for your
own welfare, wisdom which is independent of
thought appears. —HA GAKURE

❧

No man is an island, entire of itself; every man is a
piece of the continent, a part of the main.

—JOHN DONNE

❧

And whosoever of you will be the chiefest, shall be
the servant of all. —MARK 10:44

❧

The concept of an individual with a conscience is
one whose highest allegiance is to his fellow man.

—RALPH NADER

❧

Life's most urgent question is, what are you doing for others?   —MARTIN LUTHER KING, JR.

❧

No one is useless in this world who lightens the burdens of another.   —CHARLES DICKENS

❧

The purpose of the whole is to remove those who are living in this life from a state of wretchedness and lead them to the state of blessedness.

—DANTE

❧

We cannot live only for ourselves. A thousand fibers connect us with our fellow-men; and along those fibers, as sympathetic threads, our actions run as causes, and they come back to us as effects.

—HERMAN MELVILLE

❧

To work for the common good is the greatest creed.   —ALBERT SCHWEITZER

❧

We are prone to judge success by the index of our salaries or the size of our automobiles rather than by the quality of our service and relationship to mankind. —MARTIN LUTHER KING, JR.

❧

A man's value to the community primarily depends on how far his feelings, thoughts, and actions are directed towards promoting the good of his fellows.

—ALBERT EINSTEIN

❧

Mankind's role is to fulfill his heaven-sent purpose through a sincere heart that is in harmony with all creation and loves all things.

—MORIHEI UESHIBA

❧

The true meaning of life is to plant trees, under whose shade you do not expect to sit.

—NELSON HENDERSON

❦

When people are serving, life is no longer meaning-less.
                                        —JOHN GARDNER

❦

An individual has not started living until he can rise above the narrow confines of individualistic concerns to the broader concerns of all humanity.
                         —MARTIN LUTHER KING, JR.

❦

It is more important to find out what you are giving to society than to ask what is the right means of livelihood.
                                  —J. KRISHNAMURTI

❦

To have a great purpose to work for, a purpose larger than ourselves, is one of the secrets of making life significant, for then the meaning and worth of the individual overflow his personal borders and survive his death.
                                        —WILL DURANT

❦

I am never weary of being useful. . . . In serving others I cannot do enough. No labor is sufficient to tire me. ——LEONARDO DA VINCI

❧

Whosoever shall seek to save his life shall lose it; and whosoever shall lose his life shall preserve it.

——LUKE 17:33

❧

Consciously or unconsciously, every one of us does render some service or other. If we cultivate the habit of doing this service deliberately, our desire for service will steadily grow stronger, and will make, not only for our own happiness, but that of the world at large. ——MAHATMA GANDHI

THE
ART
OF
ZEN

The art of Zen is the art of life. Life is a creative process and best lived as one. In our creating, we have the opportunity to bring love, beauty, attention, and joy to all we do. The art of Zen begins with the recognition that our experience of life is what we make of it. Life can be a dreary struggle for survival, a frantic chase for wealth and goods, a desperate search for recognition and approval—or it can be a creative art.

The word *art* comes from a Latin root meaning "to arrange." We can think of an artist in any field as a master arranger. The creative life produces beautiful arrangements, not by imposing a rational or conceptual order on things, but by penetrating to their essence and working in harmony with the order inherent in nature. A life lived as art is triumphant and heroic, yet filled with the deepest humility. It recognizes the spiritual reality of Oneness, while at the same time delighting in the uniqueness of multiplicity, the Ten Thousand Things. When we are at one with the Creative Principle, we recognize that the universe is for us and with us, and we allow it to do what it is doing through us, without resisting or holding on.

❧

The truth of Zen, just a little bit of it, is what turns one's humdrum life, a life of monotonous, uninspiring commonplaceness, into one of art, full of genuine inner creativity.   —D. T. SUZUKI

❧

Art is the proper task of life.

—FRIEDRICH NIETZSCHE

❧

Artists in each of the arts seek after and care for nothing but love.   —MARSILIO FICINO

❧

The work of art is above all a process of creation, it is never experienced as a mere product.

—PAUL KLEE

❧

For man is by nature an artist.   —TAGORE

❧

The greatest productions of art, whether painting, music, sculpture or poetry, have invariably this quality—something approaching the work of God.

—D. T. SUZUKI

❧

Industry without art is brutality.

—ANANDA K. COOMARASWAMY

❧

Construction on a purely spiritual basis is a slow business . . . The artist must train not only his eye but also his soul . . .   —WASSILY KANDINSKY

❧

Everywhere I go I find a poet has been there
before me. —SIGMUND FREUD

✿

Thoroughly to know oneself, is above all art, for it
is the highest art. —THEOLOGIA GERMANICA

✿

Where the spirit does not work with the hand there
is no art. —LEONARDO DA VINCI

✿

The art of life, of a poet's life, is, not having anything to do, to do something.

—HENRY DAVID THOREAU

✿

The way of the mystic and the way of the artist are
related, except that the mystic doesn't have the
craft. —JEAN ERDMAN

✿

The secret of art is love.

—ANTOINE BOURDELLE

✺

The Whole Business of Man Is The Arts, & All
Things Common. —WILLIAM BLAKE

✺

A craft can only have meaning when it serves a
spiritual way. —TITUS BURCKHARDT

✺

Art may improve, but cannot surpass nature.
—MIGUEL DE CERVANTES

✺

The productions of all arts are kinds of poetry and
their craftsmen are all poets. —PLATO

✺

In the world of art, our consciousness being freed
from the tangle of self-interest, we gain an unob-
structed vision of unity, the incarnation of the real,
which is a joy for ever. —TAGORE

✺

Imagination, not invention, is the supreme master of
life.
—JOSEPH CONRAD

❧

The excellency of every art is in its intensity,
capable of making all disagreeables evaporate.
—KEATS

❧

In every block of marble I see a statue as plain as
though it stood before me, shaped and perfect in attitude and action. I have only to hew away the
rough walls that imprison the lovely apparition to
reveal it to other eyes as mine see it.
—MICHELANGELO

❧

Art is not an end in itself, but a means of address-
ing humanity.
—M. P. MOUSSORGSKI

❧

The artist does not see things as they are, but as
he is.
—ALFRED TONNELLE

PERSEVERANCE

For every worthwhile goal, as the *I Ching* so often reminds us, "Perseverance furthers." Opportunities for the greatest practical and spiritual breakthroughs come when we have reached the absolute limits of our energies and abilities and somehow manage to push through. Perseverance requires equal parts commitment to purpose and detachment from results. Commitment to purpose keeps us moving forward into the attitudes and activities that serve to fulfill it. Detachment from results keeps us from becoming frustrated and discouraged when things don't immediately work out as we had hoped. Perseverance, then, is balance of masculine and feminine energies, an aggressive forward thrust into activity and a patient, steady endurance.

Exhorting the value of consistent daily application, my Zen teacher would often say, "One by one, day by day." Whether it is our spiritual training or the requirements of the creative process of doing and making, the temptation is always there to give up too easily and too soon. We tend to be greedy for results, overeager to arrive at our desired destinations. It helps to remind ourselves that the means are the ends; the journey, the destination. As often as not, success comes to those who ignore their setbacks and simply refuse to give up.

❧

Nothing great is created suddenly, any more than a bunch of grapes or a fig. —EPICTETUS

❧

Nothing in the world can take the place of persistence. Talent will not; nothing is more common than unsuccessful men with talent. Genius will not; unrewarded genius is almost a proverb. Education will not; the world is full of educated derelicts. Persistence and determination alone are omnipotent.

—CALVIN COOLIDGE

❧

One of the simplest things about all the facts of life is that to get where you want to go, you must keep on keeping on. —NORMAN VINCENT PEALE

❧

Be patient toward all that is unresolved in your heart and try to love the *questions themselves*. . . .

—RAINER MARIA RILKE

❧

If you care enough for the result, you will almost always attain it. —WILLIAM JAMES

❧

God is with those who persevere. —THE KORAN

❧

A lot of successful people are risk-takers. Unless you are willing to do that, to have a go, to fail miserably, and have another go, success won't happen. —PHILLIP ADAMS

❧

Go confidently in the direction of your dreams. Act
as though it were impossible to fail.

—DORTHEA BRANDT

❧

Do not think that what is hard for thee to master is
impossible for man; but if a thing is possible and
proper to man, deem it attainable by thee.

—MARCUS AURELIUS

❧

Those who reach greatness on earth reach it
through concentration.   —UPANISHADS

❧

The great secret of success is to go through life as
a man who never gets used to failing.

—ALBERT SCHWEITZER

❧

Life can be pulled by goals just as surely as it can
be pushed by drives.   —VIKTOR FRANKL

❧

Thousands of people have talent. I might as well congratulate you for having eyes in your head. The one and only thing that counts is: Do you have staying power? —NOEL COWARD

❧

If you must begin then go all the way, because if you begin and quit, the unfinished business you have left behind begins to haunt you all the time.

—CHÖGYAM TRUNGPA

❧

It's not the size of the dog in a fight, it's the size of the fight in the dog. —KIT RAYMOND

❧

I hold to the doctrine that with ordinary talent, and extraordinary perseverance, all things are attainable.

—THOMAS BUXTON

❧

Perseverance is a great element of success. If you only knock long enough and loud enough at the gate, you are sure to wake up somebody.

—HENRY LONGFELLOW

❧

That which we persist in doing becomes easier—not that the nature of the task has changed, but an ability to do it has increased.

—RALPH WALDO EMERSON

❧

Steady perseverance alone will tame your mind, and it is only through a tame mind that you can experience God. —SATHYA SAI BABA

❧

The man of virtue makes the difficulty to be overcome his first business, and success only a subsequent consideration. —CONFUCIUS

❧

There is no royal road to anything. One thing at a time, and all things in succession. That which grows slowly endures. —JOSHUA HOLLAND

※

Great works are performed not by strength but by perseverance. —SAMUEL JOHNSON

LETTING

GO

We can speak of letting go in two respects: letting go in the moment and a deeper letting go, or surrender, of the ego. Letting go in the moment comes with the acceptance of insecurity, the realization that since life is constantly changing, there is nothing to hold onto. Holding onto happiness is one of the surest ways of making ourselves miserable. In fact, the only better way is holding onto misery itself. Each moment has its own lessons, joys, and sorrows, which can only be fully experienced when we give up trying to be in control and let go into the changes.

On a deeper level, letting go means releasing attachment to the ego. The life of Zen requires giving up the notion that the desires of our separative egos will ever make us happy. It is not the failure to fulfill these desires that brings unhappiness. It is the desires themselves. In Buddhism, they are referred to as cravings (*trishnā*) and are considered to be the origin of all human suffering.

In a universe of Oneness, the ego struggles to maintain the illusion of a separate existence. In truth, letting go of the ego and letting go of struggle are one and the same. When, once and for all, we give up the struggle to prove that we are worthy of love or approval, the struggle to justify our existence, the struggle to hold onto limited beliefs and concepts of how things should be—we free ourselves to enjoy life as it is.

❧

People wish to be settled. Only as far as they are unsettled is there any hope for them.

—RALPH WALDO EMERSON

❧

It is only when we realize that life is taking us nowhere that it begins to have meaning.

—P. D. OUSPENSKY

❧

There is no security in life, only opportunity.

—MARK TWAIN

❧

Everything is in flux. —HERACLITUS

❧

My hopes must no more change their name.

—WILLIAM WORDSWORTH

❧

Consistency is contrary to nature, contrary to life.
The only completely consistent people are the dead.

—ALDOUS HUXLEY

❧

A foolish consistency is the hobgoblin of little
minds . . . With consistency, a great soul has
simply nothing to do.

—RALPH WALDO EMERSON

❧

Everything flows on and on like this river, without
pause, day and night.   —CONFUCIUS

❧

Life can be understood backwards; but it must be
lived forwards.   —SÖREN KIERKEGAARD

❧

Truly, because of our accepting and rejecting, we
have not the suchness of things.   —SENG-T'SAN

❧

You must lose a fly to catch a trout.

—GEORGE HERBERT

❧

As you watch it, your life turns to dust.   —KABIR

❧

Wisdom is oftentimes nearer when we stoop
Than when we soar.

—WILLIAM WORDSWORTH

✖

No man enjoys the true taste of life but he who is
ready and willing to quit it. —SENECA

✖

Do not cherish the unworthy desire that the
changeable might become the unchanging.

—BUDDHA

MEDITATION

There is a Zen saying attributed to an unknown ancient: "In Zen the important thing is to stop the course of the mind." The "purpose" of meditation is to do precisely this—stop the course of the mind. It is the still mind, not the formal practice of meditation, that counts. Meditation is not to be clung to as a goal unto itself nor displayed as a badge of spiritual merit. It is rather a means to be employed to tame the mind—to stop the flow of automatic subconscious thinking. (Though in the best of the Zen tradition, even this sense of purposefulness is rejected in favor of "sitting just to sit.") Once a quietness of mind has been achieved, there is no longer any need for formal meditation. As a Zen saying goes, "When we have crossed to the other shore, what need have we of a boat?" Indeed now one has become an amphibian, his life an ongoing meditation, whether moving in the land of action or resting in the sea of being.

The modern Japanese Zen tradition has come to rely on two types of meditation: the *koan*, a kind of question or puzzle that essentially uses the mind to exhaust the mind, and sitting meditation, or *zazen*. The *Rinzai* school emphasizes the *koan*, while the *Soto* school puts its emphasis on *zazen*. In the practice of *zazen*, attention to the breath is the key. Simply by sitting still and watching its movement, the breath returns to its natural flow or "original source." As the breath becomes deep, full, and easy, the mind becomes still.

ɞ

All human evil comes from a single cause, man's inability to sit still in a room.   —BLAISE PASCAL

ɞ

Contemplation for an hour is better than formal worship for sixty years.   —MOHAMMED

❦

If you can't meditate in a boiler room, you can't
meditate. —ALAN WATTS

❦

We become contemplative when God discovers
Himself in us. —THOMAS MERTON

❦

Your mind is the cycle of births and death.
—SRI RAMANA MAHARSHI

❦

Stop thinking that meditation is anything special.
Stop thinking altogether. —SURYA SINGER

❦

Look within, and in a flash you will conquer the
Apparent and the Void. —SENG-T'SAN

❦

It is a mistake to think that the sādhnā cannot be
practiced for lack of time. The real cause is agita-
tion of the mind. —SWĀMI BRAHMĀNANDA

✿

It is essential that the mind and the body become
motionless. ——HSIEH TAO-KUANG

✿

Those who seek the truth by means of intellect and
learning only get further and further away from it.
——HUANG-PO

✿

The highest yoga is the control of the mind.
——SRIMAD BHAGAVATAM

✿

In the loving introversion of the just man all venial
sins are like to drops of water in a glowing furnace.
——JAN VAN RUYBROECK

✿

He who has exhausted all his mental constitution
knows his nature. Knowing his nature, he knows
heaven. ——MENCIUS

&

For the Great Spirit is everywhere; He hears whatever is in our minds and hearts, and it is not necessary to speak to Him in a loud voice.

—BLACK ELK

&

Silence is the garden of meditation.   —ALĪ

&

Seeking the Mind with the mind,—is not this the
greatest of all mistakes?   —SENG-T'SAN

&

When you understand it's foolish to look for fire with
    fire,
The meal is already cooked.

—WU-MEN

&

A mind that is fast is sick. A mind that is slow is
sound. A mind that is still is divine.

—MEHER BABA

❧

All of the significant battles are waged within the
self.   —SHELDON KOPP

❧

Look at that battle you are involved in; you are
caught in it: you are it.   —J. KRISHNAMURTI

❧

In the Buddha Dharma, practice and realization are
identical.   —DŌGEN

❧

The heart of the ordinary unenlightened man,
because of his surroundings, is always liable to
change, just like monkeys jumping from one branch
to another. It is indeed in a state of confusion,
easily moved and with difficulty controlled.

        —HŌNEN

❧

The seed of mystery lies in muddy water.
How can I perceive this mystery?
Water becomes clear through stillness.

How can I become still?
By flowing with the stream.

—LAO-TZU

✿

Be still, and know that I am God.

—PSALMS 46:10

✿

If you ask him: "What is silence?" he will answer:
"It is the Great Mystery! The holy silence is His
voice!" If you ask: "What are the fruits of
silence?" he will say: "They are self-control, true
courage or endurance, patience, dignity, and rever-
ence. Silence is the cornerstone of character."

—OHIYESA

✿

When the soul has stripped away all comprehensible
things, it is left with God, the incomprehensible.

—ST. ALONSO

MINDFULNESS

When asked, "What is Zen?" a master replied: "Attention! Attention! Attention!" Mindfulness is nothing more or less than the practice of attention. Zen wants us to wake from the sleepwalk of the routine and automatic—to bring full attention to our walking and talking, hearing and breathing, eating and working, indeed, to every aspect of our lives.

Zen recognizes that awareness transforms experience. There is no right or wrong way of doing things; there is only being more or less conscious. In the practice of mindfulness, the goal, if you can call it that, is not to correct ourselves but to become more fully conscious of ourselves. Because they rely on memory, efforts at self-correction are always removed from the immediacy of the moment. Instead of struggling to improve ourselves, we can bring attention to the way we view the world around us and to our reactions and responses to it. Experienced mindfully, even the most sordid human passions, which many religious traditions seek to erase through force of will, become vehicles for liberation.

For example, when a thought of jealousy arises, we can unconsciously give way to it and be quickly overtaken by hatred. We can struggle against it, telling ourselves, "I shouldn't think this," and get caught up in guilt. Or we can examine the thought itself and attempt to understand the context from which it has arisen. What views of life, the universe, and myself am I holding that prompt me to see myself threatened by the good of another? In this way, even our basest thoughts and feelings become windows to awakening.

❧

It is far more important that one's life should be perceived than that it should be transformed; for no sooner has it been perceived, than it transforms itself of its own accord.

—MAURICE MAETERLINCK

❧

The aim of life is to live, and to live means to be awake, joyously, drunkenly, serenely, divinely aware. ——HENRY MILLER

❧

It is our less conscious thoughts and our less conscious actions which mainly mould our lives and the lives of those who spring from us.

——SAMUEL BUTLER

❧

Again and again, look within thine own mind.

——PADMA-SAMBHAVA

❧

Be still and cool in thy own mind and spirit.

——GEORGE FOX

❧

Within our impure mind the pure one is to be found. ——HUI-NENG

❦

Nothing divides one so much as thought.

—R. H. BLYTH

❦

There is some soul of goodness in things evil,
would men observingly distill it out.

—SHAKESPEARE

❦

Zen is mind-less activity, that is, Mind-ful activity,
and it may often be advisable to emphasize the
mind, and say, "Take care of the thoughts and the
actions will take care of themselves."

—R. H. BLYTH

❦

You wish to see; Listen. Hearing is a step toward
Vision.
—ST. BERNARD

❦

When the will and the imagination are in conflict, it
is always the imagination that wins.

—ÉMILLE COUÉ

❧

Use every means all through the day to guard your
samadhi-power as you would protect a child.

—DŌGEN

❧

One who has attained the Tao is master of himself,
and the universe is dissolved for him. Throw him
in the company of the noisy and the dirty, and he
will be like a lotus flower growing from muddy
water, touched by it, yet unstained.   —T'U LUNG

❧

Awaken the mind without fixing it anywhere.

—DIAMOND SUTRA

❧

The first rule is to keep an untroubled spirit. The
second is to look things in the face and know them
for what they are.   —MARCUS AURELUIS

❧

Compared to what we ought to be, we are half
awake.   —WILLIAM JAMES

ENLIGHTENMENT

Zen does not like to speak of enlightenment. Yet it must. It is the paradox revealed in the famous saying by the Taoist master Lao-tzu: "Those who know do not speak and those who speak do not know." Yet why say even this? The difficulty comes in trying to communicate the ineffable, to explain the unexplainable. There is always the possibility, indeed, the likelihood, of getting caught in a net of words or lost in a labyrinth of concepts and missing the Reality they are pointing at. This is the paradox: To say nothing shows lack of compassion; to say too much risks leading astray.

Consequently, when speaking of enlightenment, "the Buddha," or reality, Zen masters rely on "direct pointing." Direct pointing may take the form of

abrupt physical actions or irrational statements that
pitch the questioner out of intellect and into the "suchness" of things. "What is the Buddha?" T'ung-shan
was asked. His reply: "Three pounds of flax." You
can't figure it out. But if your own experience has
made you sufficiently ripe, you may, with just a nudge,
behold the sun through the clouds of unknowing.

❧

The wisdom of enlightenment is inherent in every
one of us. It is because of the delusion under which
our mind works that we fail to realize it ourselves,
and that we have to seek the advice and the
guidance of enlightened ones.　　　－－HUI-NENG

❧

Illusion produces rest and motion. Illumination destroys liking and disliking.　　　－SENG-T'SAN

❧

To the man of realization . . . it is indifferent
whether the senses . . . are indrawn or turned
without. What matters it to the sun whether the
clouds gather together or are dispersed?

　　　－SRIMAD BHAGAVATAM

❧

Not knowing how near the truth is,
People seek it far away, what a pity!
They are like him who, in the midst of water,
Cries in thirst so imploringly.

—HAKUIN

❧

Never, my son, can a soul that has so far uplifted
itself as to grasp the truly good and real slip back
to the evil and unreal. —HERMES

❧

There is no need to wait until another life or for
future generations. Before you is the Buddha who
proves to you the possibility of penetrating to God.

—CHANG PO-TUAN

❧

He who knows others is wise;
He who knows himself is enlightened.

—LAO-TZU

❧

Thou shalt know God without image and without
means.   ——MEISTER ECKHART

*

Underlying great doubt there is great satori, where
there is thorough questioning there will be thor-
oughgoing experience of awakening.

——ZEN SAYING

*

The reward of all action is to be found in enlightenment.   ——BHAGAVAD-GITA

*

When people reach the highest perfection, it is
nothing special; it is their normal condition.

——HINDU SAYING

*

Since I received enlightenment in the infinite
wonders of truth I have always been cheerful and
laughing.   ——HUNG CH'ENG-CH'OU

*

Realize they Simple Self,
Embrace thy Original Nature.

—LAO-TZU

❧

Before enlightenment, I chopped wood and carried
water; after enlightenment, I chopped wood and
carried water.   —ZEN SAYING

❧

The attainment of enlightenment from the ego's
point of view is extreme death.

—CHÖGYAM TRUNGPA

❧

Those who really seek the path to Enlightenment
dictate terms to their mind. They then proceed with
strong determination.   —BUDDHA

❧

Satori [enlightenment] is the *raison d'être* of Zen,
and without it there is no Zen.   —D. T. SUZUKI

❧

It is characteristic of the ego that it takes all that is
unimportant as important and all that is important
as unimportant.   —MEHER BABA

🐦

When we're not attached to anything, all things are
   as they are:
With activity there is no going, no staying.
                                  —SENG-T'SAN

🐦

Vast emptiness, nothing sacred.   —BODHIDHARMA

🐦

Outside mind there is no Buddha,
Outside Buddha, there is no mind.
Do not cling to good,
Do not reject evil!

      —MA-TSU

All the fish needs
Is to get lost in the water
All man needs is to get lost
In Tao.

—CHUANG-TZU

EVERYDAY

ZEN

Zen is not religion. Neither is it something lofty or remote. If we were to say anything about what Zen "is," we could say that it is the poetry of life. Everyday life. The familiar Zen saying, "Before enlightenment, I chopped wood and carried water; after enlightenment, I chopped wood and carried water," tells us all we need to know.

Zen is nothing special. It is meeting our everyday responsibilities with energy and cheerfulness. It is embracing the gift of life and enjoying the beauty of simple things and activities. It is maintaining a lightness and calm, a sense of humor and play as we go about our everyday business.

Everyday Zen means dealing with the world as it

is, not insisting that it be the way we think it should be before we will love and embrace it. The greed, the violence, the pettiness, the stupidity we see all around us—these cry out for our love and understanding, not our condemnation. Condemnation never changed anything for the better.

If in a selfish world I remain compassionate, in a violent world I remain peaceful, in a shallow world I maintain depth and sincerity, in a world of ingratitude I celebrate the gift of life, then I have done what I can do. A Zen attitude frees us from ideas of victimization that permeate popular culture and reminds us that we are the "them" we so often complain about. It says, Don't spend your time in idle complaint; roll up your sleeves and get to work.

❦

The Way is not far from man; if we take the Way as something superhuman, beyond man, this is not the real Way.   —CONFUCIUS

❦

Your everyday mind—that is the Way!
                                    —UNMON BUN'EN

❧

Although profoundly "inconsequential," the Zen experience has consequences in the sense that it may be applied in any direction, to any conceivable human activity, and that wherever it is so applied it lends an unmistakable quality to the work.

—ALAN WATTS

❧

It is preoccupation with possessions, more than anything else, that prevents us from living freely and nobly.   —BERTRAND RUSSELL

❧

I have not the shadow of a doubt that any man or woman can achieve what I have, if he or she would make the same effort and cultivate the same hope and faith.   —MAHATMA GANDHI

❧

One cannot always be a hero, but one can always be a man.   —JOHANN GOETHE

❦

Simplify! ——HENRY DAVID THOREAU

❦

Everybody can be great. Because everyone can serve . . . You only need a heart full of grace. A soul generated by love.

——MARTIN LUTHER KING, JR.

❦

The power of man's virtue should not be measured by his special efforts, but by his ordinary doings.

——BLAISE PASCAL

❦

Too many people spend money they haven't earned, to buy things they don't want, to impress people they don't like. ——WILL ROGERS

❦

Earth provides enough to satisfy every man's need, but not every man's greed. ——MAHATMA GANDHI

❧

What is particularly intriguing, in fact, is that whereas many peoples tend to locate this experience [of the sacred] in certain unusual, if not "supernatural" moments and circumstances . . . the Oriental focus is upon mystery in the most obvious, ordinary, mundane—the most natural--situations of life. —CONRAD HYERS

❧

Zen is not some kind of excitement, but concentration on our usual everyday routine.

—SHUNRYU SUZUKI

❧

The more a man lays stress on false possessions, and the less sensitivity he has for what is essential, the less satisfying is his life. —CARL JUNG

❧

Life is like playing a violin in public and learning the instrument as one goes along.

—SAMUEL BUTLER

❧

What, then, is your duty? What the day demands.

—JOHANN GOETHE

❧

Nothing would be done at all if a man waited until he could do it so well that no one could find fault with it. —CARDINAL NEWMAN

❧

Life's a tough proposition, and the first hundred years are the hardest. —WILSON MIZNER

❧

Do not wait for the last judgment, it takes place every day. —ALBERT CAMUS

❧

A man travels the world over in search of what he needs and returns home to find it.

—GEORGE MOORE

❧

When you're both alive and dead,
Thoroughly dead to yourself,
How superb the smallest pleasure!
　　　　　　　—BU'NAN SHIDO

❧

A noble person attracts noble people, and knows
how to hold onto them.　　　—JOHANN GOETHE

❧

There is nothing so easy but that it becomes difficult when you do it reluctantly.　　　—TERENCE

❧

Every minute you are angry, you lose sixty seconds
of happiness.　　　—RALPH WALDO EMERSON

❧

For everything that lives is holy, life delights in
life . . .　　　—WILLIAM BLAKE

❧

Love truth, but pardon error. —VOLTAIRE

❧

There's no cure for birth and death save to enjoy
the interval. —GEORGE SANTAYANA

❧

One word frees us of all the weight and pain of
life: that word is love. —SOPHOCLES

❧

The best thing about the future is that it comes
only one day at a time. —ABRAHAM LINCOLN

❧

If we walk
The true Way
In our inmost heart,
Even without praying,
God will be with us!
        —TAKUAN

FOR THE BEST IN PAPERBACKS, LOOK FOR THE

Available from Laurence G. Boldt and Penguin Books

☐ **ZEN AND THE ART OF MAKING A LIVING**
A Practical Guide to Creative Career Design
For career consultant Laurence Boldt, everyone is the artist of his or her own life. In this potentially life-changing book, he offers the most innovative, unconventional—and profoundly practical—career guide since *What Color is Your Parachute?* In addition to more traditional material like assessing skills and writing a résumé, there is a wealth of information not generally found in career guides, including how to start a business, work freelance, found a non-profit corporation—and love what you are doing until you're doing what you love.

ISBN 0-14-019469-X

☐ **HOW TO FIND THE WORK YOU LOVE**
Technological advances and the global marketplace are changing the way we work and live. Now, more than ever, the importance of—and chances of—finding a job one truly loves are increasing. Laurence Boldt has reduced the quest for meaningful work to its essence, and will lead readers toward a breakthrough understanding of what they could and should be doing with their lives.

ISBN 0-14-019524-6

• ALSO AVAILABLE ON AUDIOCASSETTE FROM PENGUIN AUDIOBOOKS

☐ **ZEN SOUP**
Tasty Morsels of Wisdom from Great Minds East & West
This book of inspirational quotations from philosophers, religious leaders, and popular figures throughout history will inspire and enlighten readers. Each chapter opens with an entertaining and informative essay on a variety of topics followed by sage advice from the great minds of history. You'll find Lao Tzu on courage, Colette on joy, and Flip Wilson on living in the moment. *Zen Soup* is an invaluable source of wisdom for anyone looking for meaning in this world.

ISBN 0-14-01-9560-2

FOR THE BEST IN PAPERBACKS, LOOK FOR THE

In every corner of the world, on every subject under the sun, Penguin represents quality and variety—the very best in publishing today.

For complete information about books available from Penguin—including Puffins, Penguin Classics, and Arkana—and how to order them, write to us at the appropriate address below. Please note that for copyright reasons the selection of books varies from country to country.

In the United Kingdom: Please write to *Dept. JC, Penguin Books Ltd, FREEPOST, West Drayton, Middlesex UB7 0BR.*

If you have any difficulty in obtaining a title, please send your order with the correct money, plus ten percent for postage and packaging, to *P.O. Box No. 11, West Drayton, Middlesex UB7 0BR*

In the United States: Please write to *Consumer Sales, Penguin USA, P.O. Box 999, Dept. 17109, Bergenfield, New Jersey 07621-0120.* VISA and MasterCard holders call 1-800-253-6476 to order all Penguin titles

In Canada: Please write to *Penguin Books Canada Ltd, 10 Alcorn Avenue, Suite 300, Toronto, Ontario M4V 3B2*

In Australia: Please write to *Penguin Books Australia Ltd, P.O. Box 257, Ringwood, Victoria 3134*

In New Zealand: Please write to *Penguin Books (NZ) Ltd, Private Bag 102902, North Shore Mail Centre, Auckland 10*

In India: Please write to *Penguin Books India Pvt Ltd, 706 Eros Apartments, 56 Nehru Place, New Delhi 110 019*

In the Netherlands: Please write to *Penguin Books Netherlands bv, Postbus 3507, NL-1001 AH Amsterdam*

In Germany: Please write to *Penguin Books Deutschland GmbH, Metzlerstrasse 26, 60594 Frankfurt am Main*

In Spain: Please write to *Penguin Books S.A., Bravo Murillo 19, 1° B, 28015 Madrid*

In Italy: Please write to *Penguin Italia s.r.l., Via Felice Casati 20, I-20124 Milano*

In France: Please write to *Penguin France S.A., 17 rue Lejeune, F–31000 Toulouse*

In Japan: Please write to *Penguin Books Japan, Ishikiribashi Building, 2–5–4, Suido, Bunkyo-ku, Tokyo 112*

In Greece: Please write to *Penguin Hellas Ltd, Dimocritou 3, GR–106 71 Athens*

In South Africa: Please write to *Longman Penguin Southern Africa (Pty) Ltd, Private Bag X08, Bertsham 2013*